LEARNING NEW

How To Books on Jobs and Careers

Applying for a Job
Career Networking
Career Planning for Women
Finding a Job in Canada
Finding a Job in Computers
Finding a Job with a Future
Finding Work Overseas
Freelance DJ-ing
Freelance Teaching & Tutoring
Getting Into Films and Television
Getting Your First Job
How to Apply for a Job
How to Be a Freelance Journalist
How to Be a Freelance Sales Agent
How to Be a Freelance Secretary
How to Become an Au Pair
How to Do Voluntary Work Abroad
How to Find Temporary Work Abroad
How to Get a Job Abroad
How to Get a Job in America
How to Get a Job in Australia
How to Get a Job in Europe
How to Get a Job in France
How to Get a Job in Germany
How to Get a Job in Travel & Tourism
How to Get Into Radio
How to Get That Job
How to Know Your Rights at Work
How to Manage Your Career
How to Market Yourself
How to Return to Work
How to Start a New Career
How to Work from Home
How to Work in an Office
How to Work in Retail
How to Work with Dogs
How to Write a CV That Works
Learning New Job Skills
Living & Working in China
Passing That Interview
Surviving Redundancy
Working as a Holiday Rep
Working in Hotels & Catering
Working in Japan
Working in Photography
Working on Contract Worldwide
Working on Cruise Ships
Working with Children
Working with Horses

Other titles in preparation

The How To Series now contains more than 200 titles in the following categories:

Business Basics
Family Reference
Jobs & Careers
Living & Working Abroad
Student Handbooks
Successful Writing

Please send for a free copy of the latest catalogue for full details (see back cover for address).

How To Books

JOBS & CAREERS

LEARNING NEW JOB SKILLS

How and where to obtain the right training to help you get on at work

Laurel Alexander

How To Books

By the same author in this series

Career Networking
Career Planning for Women
Surviving Redundancy

Cartoons by Mike Flanagan

British Library Cataloguing in Publication Data
A catalogue record for this book is available from the British Library.

© Copyright 1997 by Laurel Alexander.

Published by How To Books Ltd, 3 Newtec Place, Magdalen Road, Oxford, OX4 1RE, United Kingdom. Tel: (01865) 793806. Fax: (01865) 248780.

All rights reserved. No part of this work may be reproduced or stored in an information retrieval system (other than for purposes of review) without the express permission of the Publisher in writing.

Note: The material contained in this book is set out in good faith for general guidance and no liability can be accepted for loss or expense incurred as a result of relying in particular circumstances on statements made in the book. The laws and regulations are complex and liable to change, and readers should check the current position with the relevant authorities before making personal arrangements.

Produced for How To Books by Deer Park Productions.
Typeset by PDQ Typesetting, Stoke-on-Trent, Staffs.
Printed and bound by Cromwell Press, Broughton Gifford, Melksham, Wiltshire.

Contents

List of illustrations 8

Preface 9

1 What can training do for me? 11

   Grasping the importance of training 11
   Ensuring your working future 11
   Training at any age 15
   Returning to the school room 15
   Getting free training 17
   Increasing confidence 17
   Case studies 18
   Discussion points 18

2 Considering jobs at the end of the training 19

   Finding a job with a future 19
   Increased demand from employers 24
   Taking an employer-led qualification 24
   Finding work 25
   Marketing your skills 26
   Case studies 29
   Discussion points 31

3 What kind of courses are available? 32

   Laying the foundations 32
   Using further education 33
   Using university 35
   Vocational training 39
   Modern apprenticeships 41
   Taking a non-qualification course 41
   Case studies 43
   Discussion points 44

4	**Paying for the training**	45
	Considering your financial obligations	45
	Finding sources of funding	45
	Obtaining welfare benefits	50
	Getting a loan	51
	Case studies	52
	Discussion points	52
5	**Coping as an adult student**	53
	Overcoming preconceptions about other students	53
	Balancing home and study	54
	Getting support	57
	Increasing your confidence	57
	Using the University of the Third Age	61
	Making experience count	61
	Case studies	61
	Discussion points	62
6	**Keeping up with the course**	63
	Remembering how you've learned	63
	Looking at your motivations	65
	Building concentration	66
	Solving problems	67
	Case studies	71
	Discussion points	71
7	**Gaining a qualification while staying at home**	72
	Defining open learning	72
	Choosing a course	73
	Open colleges	73
	Studying at home	75
	Case studies	76
	Discussion points	76
8	**Gaining a qualification and working full-time**	77
	Explaining the NVQ system	77
	Benefiting from APL	81
	Assessing competence in the workplace	83
	Finding evidence	83
	Building your portfolio	84
	Who assesses you?	84
	Case studies	85
	Discussion points	85

Contents

9 Knowing who provides the training — 87
- Understanding the TECs — 87
- Looking at industry training organisations — 87
- Overviewing business schools — 88
- Looking into further education colleges — 89
- Looking into universities — 90
- Finding other useful organisations — 90
- Case studies — 91
- Discussion points — 92

10 Making it happen — 93
- Setting your personal learning action plan — 93
- Assessing where you are now — 95
- Finding help — 97
- Moving forward — 97
- Learning for life — 98
- Case studies — 98
- Discussion points — 99

Glossary — 100

Further reading — 104

Useful addresses — 107

Index — 124

List of Illustrations

1. Stepping stones to training 16
2. Sample speculative letter 28
3. The successful interview checklist 30
4. GNVQ content 38
5. Fundamentals of GNVQs 40
6. Typical adult education courses relevant to vocational studies 42
7. Developing a networking web 56
8. Assessing a mature student's skills 58
9. Assessing a mature student's strengths 60
10. Finding what way of learning suits you 64
11. The NVQ structure 77
12. NVQs on offer 78
13. NVQ relevance to other qualifications 80
14. Breakdown of an NVQ element 82
15. Methods of assessing a candidate 82
16. Finding evidence of competence for NVQs 84
17. Benefits of NVQs 86
18. Assessing what you have already learnt 94
19. Assessing your learning, formal and informal 96
20. Plan of action 97

Preface

The changing face of work is bringing new and challenging opportunities for everyone. Gone are the days of the nine-to-five job which lasts from leaving school until retirement. Now we have the chance to have variety in our working life and learn new skills. In order to gain the most from all these changes, we need to have the relevant skills. More importantly, we need to make sure we continue to update our skills so that we can provide what employers need. Employers have specific demands which change all the time. Update your skills and make sure *you* are the one to supply the employers with what they need.

This book is about ensuring your working future. There are sections on further education, studying from home, NVQs, choosing a vocational degree and taking a non-qualification course which can help update job skills. Choosing a course is one thing, paying for it another. You may be eager and ready to learn new job skills, but the question 'how do I pay for the training?' may be holding you back. Now you can find out how to pay, or even get free training. Once you're qualified, you then want the work. Sections are included on how to find work and market your skills.

Successful learning involves more than just study skills. It is about balancing home and study and building a support network to help yourself. The book also helps you look at your motivations for learning. It will help you set learning goals so that you can make choices about the type of learning which is relevant to you.

Changing work trends mean that learning is for life. This book has been written so that you can confidently take charge of your working future and make informed decisions about learning new job skills.

Laurel Alexander

IS THIS YOU?

Unemployed   Just been made redundant

                              Mature learner

Wanting to return to study   Wanting to go to university

                         Needing to update skills

Looking for promotion   Wanting to study from home

                            Curious about NVQs

Looking for a job with a future   Career officer

                      Wanting to improve study skills

Taking an adult education course   Needing to improve your English and Maths

                       Wanting to work in business services

Hoping to work in retail   Wanting to work in education and training

                     Thinking of working in health and beauty

Seeking work in leisure and tourism   Aiming to work in science and IT

                        Wanting to work in social care

Wanting to work with the environment   Looking for residential colleges

                           Looking for a new career

Outplacement consultant   Working for Employment Services

                                  Trainer

Redundancy counsellor   Employment consultant

                            Citizens Advice worker

1
What Can Training Do for Me?

GRASPING THE IMPORTANCE OF TRAINING

Training is for everyone. We tend to associate study, learning, education and training with young people. It's what we do when we're at school or when we go to college straight from school. However, there are some fundamental differences between the four states:

- **Study** may be defined as a deliberate activity and would apply to a practical or non-practical interest.

- **Learning** may occur formally or informally and is relevant to any new situation.

- **Education** may be primarily theory based, occurring in a classroom situation, and may be linked to basic schooling or work.

- **Training** is a practical approach to learning new skills, occurring in a hands-on situation and is always linked to a working situation.

Training is a specific method of activity which improves knowledge and skills relevant to a working or vocational environment. Because of the changing face of employment, training is becoming a permanent activity which all working people need to plan for and incorporate into their working lives.

ENSURING YOUR WORKING FUTURE

Most of us are familiar with the traditional working patterns of a nine-to-five job, five days a week and retiring at 65. Whenever we wanted to change jobs, there were always several just around the corner. Nowadays, however, the world of employment is a different place.

- Short-term employment is replacing long-term and permanent jobs.

- Temporary workers are needed when companies want to increase their staff at peak times.

- The modern company is smaller, has fewer overheads and less permanent employees.

- There is an increase in self-employment as more work is contracted out to freelancers.

- More women are entering the workforce.

- Single-skilled jobs, such as manual manufacturing, are going.

- Multi-skilled workers are in demand.

- Technology is developing fast, giving rise to constant changes in working practices.

- There is an increase in service industry work.

Training has become an essential component of work, because of the increase in technology and the change in the way businesses are run. Change is happening at an incredible rate in commerce and industry. These changes produce new equipment and new processes which in turn require new skills.

Being multi-skilled
Many employers feel that young people are coming out of school and college inadequately prepared for the world of work. Even further up the line there is a shortage of adults who are properly trained in the relevant skills.

The disappearance of the single-skilled workers' jobs like typical production line work, has occurred because of improvements in technology. Now we need workers who can operate the *technology*, which in turn operates the production line. And while competition for work is becoming greater, companies are needing to cut their overheads. This means the minimum of workers, which in turn means that the workers need to be multi-skilled and/or specialists in order to be employed.

What Can Training Do for Me?

Being multi-skilled means have a number of transferable skills. For example, as an office worker, you may need to be able to operate several different computer systems, understand word processing packages and spreadsheets, know how to organise manual filing systems, be able to do audio typing, deal with difficult customers on the telephone, make travel arrangements for your boss, design promotional material, use a petty cash system and have a hundred different other skills. If you were a printer, multi-skilled would mean being able to operate several different presses and have a working knowledge of computer consoles. As a multi-skilled trainer, I can take workshops in career management, assertiveness training, word processing or even astrology.

In order to ensure your levels of skilfulness, you need training. Not just a one-off, but a periodic and constant programme of training which ensures your efficiency in your chosen trade or profession.

Providing what employers want

The basic requirements of employers are to save money and to make money. To be of maximum use to an employer, and therefore to be in work, means that you need to find out the skills they need and make sure you have them. However, it isn't enough just to get trained up in the basic skills and then think you have got it made. Because change is happening all the time, and at a fairly fast rate, you constantly need to update your skills to match the requirements of potential employers. Employers need to be able to respond to change as the market forces shift, which means you need to change and update your skills in response.

What employers want

Vocational skills	What occupational area do you specialise in?
Job-specific skills	What are the specific tasks you have experience of within the occupational area? What are you especially skilled at within your occupational area?
Interpersonal skills	How good are your communication skills? How well do you work with colleagues? Are you a good team member?
Leadership skills	Can you motivate, inspire and lead other colleagues?

Customer service skills How good are your sales skills? Can you deal with difficult customers/clients?

Developmental skills How good are you at recognising and creating opportunities for new business or increasing productivity?

It is your responsibility to make sure you are trained in the right skills, which makes you a desirable commodity to potential employers.

Increasing your earnings

As you become multi-skilled you increase your worth on the job market. Because there is no longer a job for life, you need to be able to develop the skills which you can transfer from job to job, even from occupation to occupation.

It is becoming increasingly common for people to have more than one source of income these days. Many people have what is called a **composite career**. This means they have more than one line of work. I am a career development trainer, astrologer and writer. In this day and age, when work is uncertain, it isn't always a good idea to put all your eggs in one basket.

By learning new knowledge and developing fresh skills through training, we are providing for our future. Training gives us the power to grow in experience and confidence as well as making some sort of security for our working future.

Getting out of unemployment

If you have been made redundant or your trade fluctuates, leaving you in a period of unemployment, training may offer an opportunity to change career direction or widen your existing skills.

Improving your promotional chances

If you are in work and seeking promotion, training could increase your visibility, thereby creating a favourable climate for promotional prospects.

Widening freelance opportunities

You may be considering self-employment, or maybe you want to widen your earning opportunities. Training could open the doors for you.

Taking control of your working life

We live in uncertain times. We can no longer rely on a company to be our parent and provide us with jobs, promotional prospects and a regular wage. Instead, we have to take responsibility for our own working life. We have to identify the skills required, acquire them and then market ourselves and our skills to appropriate potential employers. We need to see ourselves as the supplier, fulfilling a need to the market (the employer).

By organising a training strategy for ourselves, we can begin to take charge. We might choose to work for other people or we might want to work for ourselves. Either way, we need the right skills to do the job.

TRAINING AT ANY AGE

As a careers consultant, I work with adults who are seeking to return to the workforce or change direction. Training is always a valuable option and I have often heard clients say 'I'm too old'. Many mature people are fearful of returning to study because of the image surrounding college or university: the wrinklie among all the young people, being in a classroom again, not being able to keep up, looking silly, feeling ignorant.

The reality is that once the barriers of fear have been broken through, older students have a great deal to offer in a learning situation, maturity, wisdom, reliability and experience being just a few. In any case, training doesn't only happen in college. It is more frequently occurring in the workplace, where the real action is. As far as I am aware, the oldest student I have taken for a course was 72. She was taking a course in Word for Windows just for the sheer challenge of it.

RETURNING TO THE SCHOOLROOM

I didn't enjoy my school days. They certainly were not the best days of my life. I yawned through cookery, was always told to stand in the corridor because I talked too much and homework bored me. Now I enjoy cooking for relaxation, get paid for talking (training), and get relaxation and learning from reading factual books in my spare time. I took my first professional course in my late 20s. Why? Because I wanted to earn more money, because I wanted a more professional approach to my work and because I had a choice.

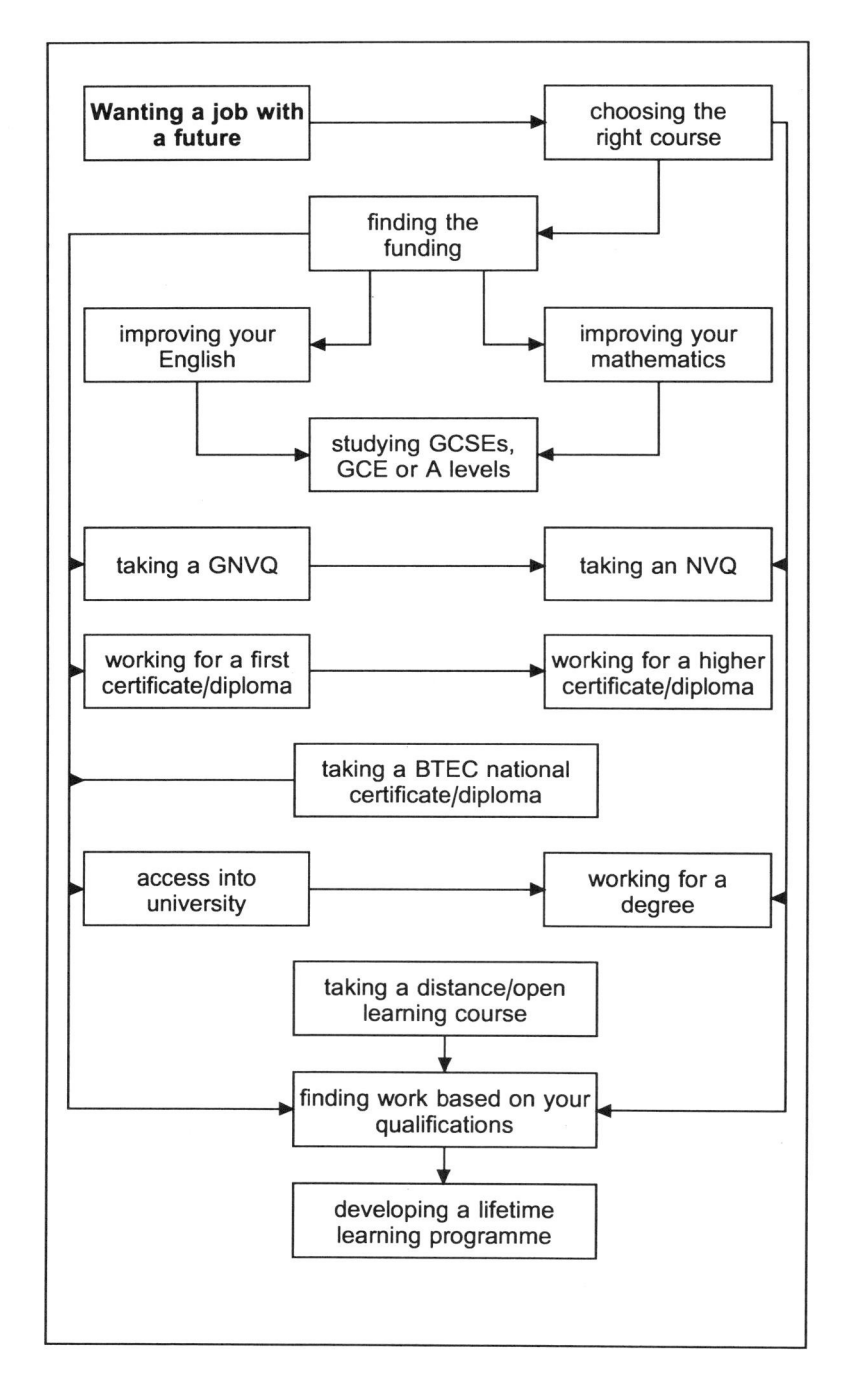

Fig. 1. Stepping stones to training.

Enjoying learning

Learning as an adult is very different from learning as a child. As children, we *have* to go to school. We may have had little or no say in the subjects we studied. Our teachers may not have been very good. Children want to have fun, not sit in rows and be told what to learn by rote. When we are adults we can *choose* what we want to learn, how we want to learn and how we experience our learning.

As an adult learner, forget the classroom. There are many new and exciting ways for you to learn new job skills. Forget about being under the control of the teacher and the system. As an adult returning to study, you have a wealth of experience to incorporate into your learning. Forget about being told off for answering back. You're an adult, exactly the same as the tutor or trainer. You're an equal now. You're returning to study to learn new skills, not to be told how to behave. You have a choice.

Training at work

There is an increase in training at work. It is becoming more common for companies to invest in a training programme for their staff. They will either have their own trainers situated within their company or they will buy in specialist training from outside.

Getting qualified at home

For some people it might not be possible to attend college full or part-time. However, it is possible to acquire new job skills from home, using **distance learning** or **open learning**.

GETTING FREE TRAINING

For people who are out of work and claiming benefit, there are free training schemes whereby it is possible to get an **NVQ (National Vocational Qualification)** plus **work experience**. It is also possible to take a qualification course at your local college for a nominal registration fee.

INCREASING CONFIDENCE

We may not always be aware of *when* we learn something. If the learning is conscious, we are driven by a mixture of need and curiosity. When we have succeeded in learning something, we feel satisfied and pleased.

To gain new knowledge or to learn new job skills, opens up our horizons of experience and increases our confidence. We have something to show off, something to sell. We have set out to learn something, gone through the learning process itself, discovered that it does work and now, in our working life, we can apply this learning. You can do it.

- 'Education's purpose is to replace an empty mind with an open one.' *Malcolm S Forbes.*

CASE STUDIES

Alan is deciding his future
Alan is 21 years old. In his last year at school he took a GNVQ in leisure just for the sake of taking something. He didn't finish it, left school and began working in the hospitality industry.

Diane wants to work from home
Diane is in her early 50s, is partially disabled with a chronic back problem and can't take a job in a normal office environment. She used to be a personal assistant with the tax office. She feels useless and depressed and wants a fresh challenge.

Tony wants a career change
Tony is in his early 40s and has worked for a major telecommunication company as an engineer for most of his working life. He is stressed out and needs a complete change.

Mel wants to manage her career
Mel is 30 and is a team leader with a major credit card company. She is very ambitious, and wants more responsibility and more money.

DISCUSSION POINTS

1. Consider your last or current job. What kind of on-the-job training did you, or do you receive?

2. Analyse the pros and cons of being multi-skilled.

3. What is the relevance of interpersonal skills in the workplace?

2
Considering Jobs at the End of the Training

FINDING A JOB WITH A FUTURE

Vocational training means taking a specific qualification for the sole purpose of paid work. I have often seen people jump with great enthusiasm into training only to find that it doesn't lead to a job. Ideally most of us would like to be working in an area which gives us pleasure and interests us. Consequently many people might take a qualification course in a subject which is riveting to them but doesn't actually fit in with the current growth areas in commerce and industry. Equally it is pointless to take up vocational training in a subject which bores you rigid. When considering a change of career direction, ask yourself:

- What are my existing skills?
- Do I want to build on my existing skills?
- Do I want to learn new skills?
- Am I considering training in a growth area of work?
- Is there likely to be relevant work following qualification?

Opportunities in social care and the protective services
According to the Careers and Occupational Information Centre:

- Field social work may be easier to find in inner cities.

- There are increasing employment opportunities in the Armed Forces as well as for independent social work agencies.

- There is an increase in the number of day centres for the elderly and disabled.

- The demand for care services is likely to grow as we become an elderly nation.

Typical job areas
Careers guidance
Fund-raising
Nursery work
Prison work
Youth work
Community work
Housing
Probation
Social work

Opportunities in education, teaching and training
- There is a demand for primary teachers in many areas.

- Secondary teachers of maths, science, modern languages, technology and business studies are needed.

- The number of training consultancies is increasing, as is the number of trainers working freelance.

According to TASC (Teaching as a Career), the trend in the increase of primary school pupils is expected to continue, which means that the demand for primary school teachers is likely to increase, with a specific need for more teachers of early-years children.

Typical job areas
Education welfare
Special educational needs
  teaching
Teaching
Further education lecturing
Teaching English as a foreign
  language
Training

Opportunities in leisure and tourism
Leisure time is increasing. In 1993 the total spent in the UK on leisure, including tourism and hospitality, was £102 billion (Local Government Management Board).
According to the Careers and Occupational Information Centre:

- The interest in photography has led to a great expansion in photofinishing services.

- Catering is a large, expanding industry.

- There will always be a demand for made-to-measure garments. There is also a shortage of skilled pattern-cutters and graders.

- Sports related openings have increased in swimming, squash, tennis, water sports, table tennis, badminton and the martial arts.

Typical job areas
Arts and entertainment
Clothing industry
Publication work
Tourism

Catering
Hotel work
Sports and recreation

Opportunities in health and beauty
According to the Careers and Occupational Information Centre:

- All branches of complementary medicine are growing.

- There has been an increase in the number of consultants directly employed by stores.

- Opportunities in continental Europe will probably increase in the next few years for dentists and dental technicians with the appropriate foreign language.

- Prospects are good for dispensing opticians willing to undertake managerial responsibilities.

- There is a demand for qualified occupational therapists which exceeds supply.

- The pharmaceutical industry has grown over recent years, with considerable advancement opportunities.

- Clinical psychology is on the increase.

According to the Institute of Food Science and Technology, the food industry has an annual turnover in excess of £50 billion, and is one of the largest employers in the United Kingdom and offers a secure career base.

Typical job areas
Acupuncture
Carework
Chiropractic
Dispensing optician work

Beauty
Chiropody
Dentistry
District nursing

Food science and technology
Herbalism
Medical research
Occupational therapy
Osteopathy
Physiotherapy
Health education
Homeopathy
Nursing
Orthotistry/prosthetistry
Pharmacy work
Psychology

Opportunities in business services and retail
- Secretaries are in demand throughout the country, especially those with information technology experience.

- There is a growing demand for people with keyboard skills, including word processor and computer operations, with audio-dictation growing in popularity.

- Opportunities are increasing in every field for qualified accounting technicians.

- The insurance underwriting and sales industry is expanding and has an increased need for staff.

- There are increasing opportunities to work on behalf of overseas clients with interests in the UK.

- Marketing opportunities exist in the consumer sector, especially fast-moving consumer goods and the overseas market.

- Opportunities for retail managers to work overseas are increasing, while the growth in self-service operation has led to increased demand for supermarket workers.

- The industrial/commercial security industry now employers more people than all the police forces in Britain, with regular vacancies.

Typical job areas
Administration and clerical
Employment agency
  consultancy
Freight forwarding
Legal profession
Management services
Retailing, wholesaling and sales
Conference organising
Finance
Language
Library/information work
Promotional services
Security

Considering Jobs at the End of the Training

Opportunities in science, engineering and IT

- There is a continual demand for qualified business machine service engineers, with an increasing number being employed by machine-hire companies offering servicing contracts.

- As the use of computers and hardware products grows, there is a steady demand for experienced personnel.

- There is likely to be an increasing need for multi-skilled engineers.

- The need for technical authors has increased as technology has advanced, and there is a shortage of authors in this country and abroad.

According to the Institute of Agricultural Engineers, improved farming and conservation techniques are urgently required in less developed countries. With an increasing world population, there is a demand for innovation.

We are spending more time inside buildings, according to the Chartered Institute of Building Service Engineers, and there is a shortage of building service personnel at all levels.

Typical job areas

Brewing	Business machine engineering
Clinical immunology	Computing
Domestic appliance servicing	Engineering
Science	Technical writing

Opportunities with the environment and animals

According to the Careers and Occupational Information Centre:

- Countryside and conservation management is a small but increasing profession.

- A growing number of personnel involved in environmental health care are being employed by hotels, retail companies and food manufacturers.

- Landscape architecture is a small but growing profession, with more vacancies in the visually unattractive areas.

- The number of riding schools is growing to meet the increased popularity of horse riding.

- Planning is a small but growing profession, with increasing openings in private practice.

The Royal Town Planning Institute reports a considerable growth in recent years of the number of planners working as planning consultants. There are increasing job opportunities in Europe, particularly for planners who are able to speak another European language.

The fish farming industry has developed rapidly within the last ten years, according to Career, Education and Training for Agriculture and the Countryside. As the traditional sea fishing industry has declined, cultivating fish for food purposes has grown.

The Institute of Horticulture says that the rapid expansion of amenity horticulture, via the garden centre industry, has an annual turnover of £2 billion and employs 30,000 people.

Typical job areas

Architecture	Countryside work
Environmental health care	Horticulture
Fish farming	Riding instructing
Surveying	Town and country planning

INCREASED DEMAND FROM EMPLOYERS

Employers are looking for people who can offer their company:

- job-specific skills
- a willingness to learn and take up training options
- flexibility of skills
- good communication skills
- customer-care skills.

The term 'job-enlargement' is becoming increasingly popular. It means that where two people used to do two jobs, now there is only one person doing both jobs. Again this means the worker needs to be multi-skilled, in order to move around a company doing a variety of work.

The more you can offer a potential employer, the more likely you are to stay in work, although not necessarily with the same company.

TAKING AN EMPLOYER-LED QUALIFICATION

Finding a job following your training period is more likely if the qualification is geared specifically towards the workplace. Employer-led qualifications fill this criteria and are called NVQs or National Vocational Qualifications. These qualifications have been put together by the lead bodies which govern the different areas of industry and commerce.

An NVQ is based upon producing evidence to show that you can do specific tasks associated with your job. The evidence is built up in three ways:

1. From being observed doing the task, either in the workplace or through a simulated activity in a training session.

2. From building up evidence, such as doing a written project or answering questions.

3. By getting written documentation from a past or current boss which confirms that you are doing, or have done, specific work-related tasks.

If you are already working, your company may allow you to improve your skills and qualifications through taking an NVQ. If you aren't working, your local college can take you through an NVQ while providing you with work experience so that you can relate the NVQ to a working environment.

NVQs are directly related to the workplace, the specific tasks and relevant knowledge necessary to do the job. There are NVQs for practically every profession and trade.

FINDING WORK

Before you embark on any training course, you need to research the potential of the job market upon completion of your qualification. Then, as you approach the end of your training course, you need to begin activating a **jobsearch strategy**.

If you are not working at the moment, due to redundancy or a career break, as well as gaining your qualification you will also need to improve your **jobsearch skills**.

Researching the job market
Research should occur before and towards the end of any training course.

Learning how to network
Developing your network skills is a crucial part of finding work at the end of your training course. Part of your training might include work experience, and this could open up more permanent opportunities following qualification.

MARKETING YOUR SKILLS

Following qualification you will need to work out a jobsearch strategy so that you can market your skills and knowledge to best advantage. When it comes to promoting yourself, did you know:

- Fifty-five per cent of your success depends upon visual factors.

- Thirty-eight per cent of your success depends on your voice.

- Seven per cent of your success depends upon your spoken word.

- Your success is decided within the first three minutes of entering the room.

Using the CV
The first step you need to take is to design and produce a basic CV. Your CV is your sales document detailing your professional background.

Tips for compiling your CV
- A CV should be no longer than two pages.

- Individually target each CV for the vacancy you are applying for.

- Have your CV word processed or typed.

- Include your full name, address and postcode, telephone number and STD code.

- If you haven't worked for some time, put a 'personal profile' at the top after your name, address and telephone number, consisting of about four sentences detailing your main skills and strengths relevant to the job you are applying for.

- Include your date of birth at the end of your CV under 'Additional'.

- If you are under 25 detail your secondary education and further education, which college and when, exams/qualifications passed.

- Detail any professional training, where and when, qualifications gained. Include any 'in-house' training or work-related adult education courses taken.

- Detail employment history, including work experience, placements, Saturday jobs, holiday work. If there are gaps in your employment history put down the years rather than the specific months. For gaps in employment put down something like 'unemployed but working in a voluntary capacity' or 'unemployed but took a course in German'. Begin with your most recent position: company, address, date from and to, responsibilities and achievements. Summarise your early working years.

- Detail hobbies, making them relevant to the position you are seeking without bending the truth too much. Add club membership or any positions of responsibility you have had as part of your interests.

- Other information may include driving licence, languages, community activities, smoker or non-smoker, able to work unsociable hours.

- Include two references from people such as teachers, tutors, ministers, doctors, youth workers, previous employers, professional people.

Sending speculative letters

There are some good reasons for writing **speculative letters**. When replying to an advertised vacancy you may be one of fifty applicants, but when you write a spec letter you may be only one of two or three people doing the same thing. Your spec letter may arrive when a vacancy needs filling but is not yet advertised; only a very small percentage of vacancies are filled through advertisements. If there is no vacancy your spec letter will show initiative and could be placed on the file for the next suitable vacancy.

Tips for sending spec letters
- Tailor-make the letters.
- The letter is a business proposition.

- Research the organisation.
- Identify in the letter where you fit in.
- Target the letter at a named individual.
- Get a meeting.
- Don't ask for a job, ask for information.
- The first paragraph of the letter should state who you are, what you do and why you are writing.
- The second paragraph is your sales pitch containing relevant skills, strengths and experience.
- The third paragraph is where you request a meeting and indicated the enclosed CV.

Print Manager101 Toytown Road
Any PressBrighton
10 Somewhere StreetSussex
London

5.8.9XTel: 01273 123456

Dear Sir

As a letterpress and litho machine minder, I am currently seeking new employment following redundancy.

I have over 25 years continuous experience covering 2 and 4-colour presses with CPC and CP Tronic. Shift and overtime hours do not present any problem and I am always willing to transfer my skills across to any unfamiliar machines.

Find enclosed my CV. Should the details be of interest, I would be happy to come in for a chat. I look forward to hearing from you.

Yours faithfully

Michael Bloggs

ENC

Fig. 2. Sample speculative letter.

Considering Jobs at the End of the Training

Completing application forms
When you apply for a job you will either be asked to send in a CV or you will be sent an application form. If you have prepared your CV the details can be transferred across to the application form.

Improving your telephone technique
When you telephone a company, either in response to an advert or on spec, your chances of selling yourself will depend on your character and enthusiasm coming across in your voice.

Tips for telephoning
- Have a clear idea of what you want from the call before dialling.
- Know the name and title of the person you want to speak to.
- Speak in a lively and enthusiastic manner (smiling helps).
- Speak firmly and clearly.
- Don't suppress your body language. Try standing up while on the phone if you want to feel more authoritative.
- Listen with your right ear to absorb facts and your left ear for extra intuition.
- Listen to the tone and pitch of voice for hidden meaning.

Going for the interview
The interview is your opportunity to sell yourself directly to a company. When people go for interviews they have a tendency to give away their power. Granted, the interviewer is the one who can hire and fire you, but equally you can vote with your feet and turn the job down. You too have power to say no or yes.

CASE STUDIES

Alan trains on the job
Alan's family are involved in catering and he used to have a Saturday job in a beach café. Although he took part of a GNVQ in leisure he didn't want to go into sports and recreation. When he left school he went to work as a bartender for a major restaurant chain. He indicated he was willing to work hard and received training while doing the job. Now he's a bar manager.

Research the company and know
what the position is about.

Ask questions.

Be enthusiastic without going overboard.

Shake hands on entering and leaving.

Look the interview/panel in the eye with a smile.

Sit relaxed in chair. Don't slouch. Don't sit forward.

Think professional.

Don't smoke.

Don't joke around, aside from pleasantries.

Take a pen and note pad out at the beginning of the
interview and make occasional notes.

Leave your coat in the reception area.

Keep your jewellery to a minimum but
wear significant earrings (or tie).

Have clean, well manicured nails with either clear or no polish.

Have clean hair, tied back or put up if appropriate.

Make up in natural, soft colours.

Carry an attaché case or leather file.

Choose neutral rather than loud colours.

Look current but not too trendy.

Avoid flashy scarves or accessories.

Wear court shoes as opposed to stilettos, flatties or boots.

Fig. 3. The successful interview checklist.

Diane is studying at home

Diane had an excellent administration and secretarial background before the accident which partially disabled her. Because she cannot sit or stand in the same position for long, she is taking private tuition in French, and book-keeping with a view to doing book-keeping for private clients at home.

Tony needs to spread his wings

Tony has received quality training from the telecommunication company he works for. However, the training is in their particular equipment and if Tony wants to transfer his skills across to a new occupation he might need wider training.

Mel wants to move out

Mel wants to get into management, but her immediate boss is a man and isn't very encouraging of her ambitions. She is considering taking a management course in her spare time, then maybe moving on to a new company.

DISCUSSION POINTS

1. The average career is said to last five years. How has your career/work path changed?

2. Looking back over your jobs, how has training, or the lack of it, influenced your effectiveness or productivity?

3. How relevant is training in jobsearch skills?

3
What Kind of Courses are Available?

LAYING THE FOUNDATIONS

Education and training comes in various guises. In this section we look at the education which usually takes place in our teens – but adults are increasingly returning to consolidate the basics – and the forms which vocational training takes.

GCSEs
This represents Key Stage 4 of the National Curriculum and offers a wide range of subjects to study. When taking GCSEs for jobs, bear in mind that some companies want A, B or C grades in maths and English (relevant to white-collar work).

GCSEs are available to adults through attending a full or part-time course at further or adult education colleges. It is also possible to study through distance learning.

GCE (AS-Level)
These are equivalent to half an A-Level. They contain half the study material and take half the time.

A-Levels
These may be used to gain access into higher education. They are available in further education and sixth form colleges.

ESOL
These initials stand for English for Speakers of Other Languages. The courses are designed to build confidence in handling English in everyday situations.

Basic education
This is useful for improving basic skills such as reading, writing and maths.

What Kind of Courses are Available?

USING FURTHER EDUCATION

Your local further education college offers a wide range of vocational courses. The following is a typical selection, taken from Brighton College of Technology's part-time prospectus for 1996/97.

ABTA Travel Agents Certificate
Aromatherapy NVQ 3
Brickwork NVQ Level 2
Business and Finance BTEC National Certificate
Catering and Hospitality Food Prep. and Cooking C and G 7242/05
Certificate in Personnel Practice (IPM)
Computer-Aided Engineering: C and G 2301 Parts 1/2/3
Direct Care NVQ Level 3
Electronics and Communication Engineering: BTEC HNC
Further and Adult Education Teachers Certificate: C and G 7306
Gardening Scheme Certificate: C and G 061
Hairdressing: NVQ Level 3
Institute of Legal Executives (Associateship)
Law (GCE A-Level)
Motor Vehicle Craft Studies: C and G 3774 + NVQ
NEBSM Certificate of Supervisory Management
Printing and Graphic Communications: C and G 5240
Reflexology: VAI Diploma
Sports Massage and Management of Sports Injuries
Training and Development Certificate
Video Production: 9231/082

Examining and awarding bodies

City and Guilds London Institute (C and G)
C and G programmes are offered in approved centres such as further education colleges. There are usually no formal entry requirements other than the discretion of the approved centre. C and G awards come in four levels:

1. Pre-vocational.
2. Occupational.
3. Career extension.
4. Senior professional.

C and G also provide NVQs.

RSA Examinations Board
Centres offering RSA qualifications include further education colleges and private training centres. The qualifications come in two categories:

1. Vocational qualifications accredited to NVQs.

2. External examinations which are set and marked directly by RSA, and structured as Stage 1 Elementary, Stage 2 Intermediate and Stage 3 Advanced.

Business Technology and Education Council (BTEC)
Qualifications are offered through further and higher education and private training centres. They offer Certificates and Diplomas, GNVQs and NVQs. These courses are a mixture of educational and work-based experience, delivered in a variety of ways such as full-time, open learning, block or day release and evening class. Their qualifications are structured over four levels:

1. First certificate/ diploma
   - the foundation is for further study the certificate is one year part-time
   - the diploma is one year full-time or two years part-time

2. National certificate/ diploma
   - skills for junior management, supervisory and technician level
   - the certificate course is two years part-time
   - the diploma is two years full-time or three years part-time
   - both are equivalent to two A-Levels

3. Higher National certificate/diploma
   - greater skills for junior management, supervisory and technician level
   - the certificate is two years part-time
   - the diploma is two years full-time or three years part-time
   - both are equivalent to a degree at pass level

4. Continuing education programme
   - modules for adults wishing to reskill.

What Kind of Courses are Available?

Scottish Vocational Education Council (SCOTVEC)
This body is responsible for developing, awarding and accrediting general vocational qualifications. They offer programmes on a part- or full-time basis at two levels of study, National Certificate and Higher National Diploma or Certificate.

London Chamber of Commerce and Industry Examination Board (LCCI)
This is one of the major examining bodies for business studies, secretarial, business English and foreign language examinations. They also offer NVQs.

College certificates and diplomas
Some colleges award their own internal certificates and diplomas.

Professional bodies
For example, the Institute of Chartered Accountants, the Law Society, the British Institute of Management.

Various examining bodies for GCSEs and A-Levels
For example, the Associated Examining Board, the Oxford and Cambridge Schools Examination Board.

USING UNIVERSITY

Qualifying for a university place

Taking entrance exams
Some institutions require potential students to sit an **entrance exam**.

Access courses
If you have no formal qualifications, **access courses** are one of the best routes to take you into university. They last between one and two years and act as a stepping stone to being offered a university place. The courses are usually offered through your local further education or sixth form college. There are a number of access courses offering different subjects, *eg* women's studies, business studies. Each course also contains elements of personal development and study skills.

A-Levels
Another stepping stone into university might be to study for A-Levels through further education, part or full-time.

Open University credits
You do not need any qualifications to do an Open University course, and completion of an OU course could provide you with **credits** which might be used as a qualification for entry to degree courses. Most higher education institutes require two credits, which may take quite a long time to get through the OU route.

Foundation course
Many higher education establishments have **foundation courses**, which may form part of the specific degree course you wish to do.

Choosing what to study at university

Higher National Certificate (HNC)
This is the part-time equivalent of the HND, taken over two years.

Higher National Diplomas (HND)
These are designed for people wanting entrance to a particular area of work including care, performing arts, engineering, computing, science, horticulture, hotels and catering, business, finance, construction, design, leisure, tourism and agriculture. They last two years full-time or three years part-time, and provide a range of academic and work-related skills.

Entry requirement is normally one A-Level, or a BTEC National Diploma or two Scottish Highers. If you have completed an access course, this could qualify you for entry.

Degrees
You could, following completion of an HND, go onto the final or second year of a related degree course or use your HND to enter a completely new degree.

First degrees
These are normally three years in length, apart from languages which are four. These degrees come at two levels:

1. **Pass degree** (Bachelor)
2. **Honours degree** first class
   second class (division 1 and 2)
   third class.

First degrees can be further categorised by the numbers of subjects studied:

- **single honours**: one main subject studied with elements of others
- **joint honours**: two subjects studied equally
- **major and minor**: two subjects studied in an unequal combination
- **modular**: a number of subjects studied which have relevance
- **combined honours**: similar to modular.

Master's degree (higher degree)
Some Bachelor's degrees can lead on to a **Master's degree**, which can be taken full-time for a year or part-time for two years.

Sandwich courses
- **thin**: includes work experience taken in three or six-month blocks throughout a four-year degree.
- **thick**: includes two years at university, then one year's employment and then one year back at university (for an HND the year's work experience comes in the middle of the two years' study).

Credit Accumulation and Transfer Schemes (CATS)
This scheme enables students to structure their course timetable in a flexible manner and gives a choice in what to study. The scheme also enables the student to leave the course at staggered stages, with qualifications relevant to the amount of completed study.

Choosing your course
Universities offer a wide range of vocational courses. The following selection is taken from the University of Sussex's Undergraduate prospectus for 1997.

BA in Applied Psychology
BSc in Biochemistry
BSc in Computer Science
BSc in Ecology and Conservation
BEng/MEng in Electronic Engineering
BA in International Relations
LLB in Law with a language
BEng in Mechanical Engineering with Business Management
BA in Media Studies with a language
MChem in Medicinal Chemistry
BSc/MPhys in Physics with Environmental Science
BEng in Robotics and Automated Manufacture
BA in Social Policy (Social Welfare).

GNVQ Foundation

3 mandatory vocational units	dealing with the basic skills and knowledge relevant to a range of occupations
3 optional units	giving the student the opportunity to study something from different vocational areas
3 core skills units (level 1)	application of number, communication and information technology

GNVQ Intermediate

4 mandatory vocational units	dealing with the basic skills and knowledge relevant to a range of occupations
2 optional units	giving the student the opportunity to study something extra
3 core skills units (level 2)	application of number, communication and information technology

GNVQ Advanced

8 mandatory vocational units	dealing with the basic skills and knowledge relevant to a range of occupations
4 optional units	giving the student the opportunity to study something extra
3 core skills units (level 3)	application of number, communication and information technology

Fig. 4. GNVQ content.

What Kind of Courses are Available?

VOCATIONAL TRAINING

These are qualifications which are employer-led, and specifically geared towards the workplace and related tasks.

GNVQs

General National Vocational Qualifications (GNVQs) are aimed primarily at young people but are suitable for adult returners. Students are required to demonstrate skills and knowledge through a series of assignments and projects. The knowledge and skills gained will serve a broad occupational area rather than focus on specific skills. GNVQs come at three levels: – **foundation** – **intermediate** – **advanced**.

Most colleges consider the entry for GNVQ Intermediate level to be one or two GCSEs and the entry to the Advanced level to be four GCSEs. Foundation and Intermediate GNVQs are designed to be full-time over one year, while an Advanced GNVQ will take two years, full-time.

GNVQs:
- are assessed outside of the workplace
- are aimed at full-time students
- develop broad vocational skills and knowledge.

GNVQ subject areas include:

landbased and environmental industries
media: communication and production
leisure and tourism
business
art and design
science
performing arts
health and social care
management studies
retail and distributive services
information technology
engineering
hospitality and catering
construction and the built environment.

NVQs

National Vocational Qualifications (NVQs) are qualifications which relate to how a job gets done (skills and knowledge). Each NVQ is put together by a **lead body**. The lead body is made up of experts from each trade and profession who draw up a list of criteria which needs to be met in order to do a job properly. There are no entry requirements and no rules about how or where you learn the skills. Candidates work at their own pace full or part-time.

Level	Entry requirements	Vocational units	Core skills units	Usual length	Relevant to
Foundation	none	3 mandatory units 3 optional from different vocational area	Level 1 in communication, application of number, and information technology	1 year	4 GCSEs 1 NVQ at level 1
Intermediate	1 or 2 GCSEs or a foundation course	4 mandatory units 2 optional units	Level 2 in communication, application of number and IT	1 year	4-5 GCSEs or 1 NVQ at level 2
Advanced	1 or 2 GCSEs or a foundation course	8 mandatory units 4 optional units	Level 3 in communication, application of number and IT	2 years	2/3 GCE A-Levels or 1 NVQ at level 3

(Adapted from *Getting into Vocational Qualifications* [*Trotman*])

Fig. 5. Fundamentals of GNVQs.

NVQs
- are primarily aimed at employees
- are assessed in the workplace
- offer qualifications in most occupational areas
- develop occupational competence.

MODERN APPRENTICESHIPS

These are aimed at the 16 and 17 year-old and last for three years. The apprentice may be employed and paid a wage or allowance while working towards an NVQ/SVQ level 3.

Accelerated modern apprenticeships

These are aimed at 18 and 19 year-olds and last about eighteen months. Training is offered for **technician, craft** and **supervisory** levels while working towards an NVQ/SVQ at level 3 or higher.

TAKING A NON-QUALIFICATION COURSE

You may feel that taking a qualification pathway is not right for you at this time. However, it is possible to study on a non-vocational course which is still helpful in improving your work prospects.

Taking an adult education class

Further education colleges have adult education sections which offer ten or twenty-week courses in a variety of subjects. These weekly courses normally last for around two hours per week and may be held during the day or in the evening. Adult education also offers Saturday workshops.

Normally there are concessions for full-time students, people who are aged 60 plus and people in receipt of unemployment benefit, family credit or income support.

Voluntary education centres
Some adult education centres are run by voluntary organisations such as the Quakers.

Using a centre for Continuing Education

These centres run part-time courses which may or may not be award-bearing. The University of Sussex, for example, now runs several award-bearing (certificate or diploma) courses in subjects such as cultural studies and landscape studies. These types of courses provide a good entry point to degree courses.

Typical adult education programme

word processing	computing
basic business skills for the self-employed	massage
	cooking
Spanish	law GCSE/A-Level
mathematics, GCSE and A/S-Level	German
	physiology GCSE
Italian	first-aid at work
sociology GCSE/A-Level	deaf sign language
emergency first-aid certificate	accounting GCSE
essential food hygiene certificate	book-keeping
counselling diploma	French
business studies A-Level	psychology GCSE/A-Level

Fig. 6. Typical adult education courses relevant to vocational studies.

The Workers' Educational Association (WEA)

This organisation offers part-time courses to adults throughout the country. It has over nine hundred local branches, each with its own programme of events.

Some points about the WEA

- WEA classes are designed to develop understanding rather than formal qualifications.

- WEA classes are open to all, not only workers.

- The classes may be during the day or evening.

- They run in cooperation with local authorities.

- The WEA works with people in deprived areas, or who suffer from social or educational disadvantage.

- They involve themselves in trade union education.

- Liberal education and higher education are part of the WEA's remit.

- They offer social and political education.

What Kind of Courses are Available?

Using volunteering as a training route
If you are unemployed you might consider voluntary work for the following reasons:

1. To keep you up to speed with your skills.
2. To get a current reference.
3. To learn new skills.
4. For current information on your CV.
5. As a way of networking back to paid work.
6. To explore a change of career.

Volunteer work might also:

1. Lead to further training.
2. Lead to a qualification.
3. Lead to paid employment in a similar field.
4. Provide opportunities to meet other people.
5. Give you a sense of achievement.
6. Give you a chance to build your self-esteem.

The demand for volunteers is rising as is the range of opportunities available. The training is usually provided free and is thorough. Many training courses might provide stepping stones to gain accredited qualifications. Look in the *Yellow Pages* for your nearest volunteer bureau. You might consider doing voluntary work in the area of:

- counselling, *eg* Samaritans or Relate

- teaching, *eg* adult literacy and numeracy

- the environment, *eg* Greenpeace

- children and young people, *eg* youth work organised by local education, Guides or Scouts

- health and social care, *eg* hospitals, social service departments.

CASE STUDIES

Alan is going for silver
Alan works for a major name in the hospitality industry which has its own in-house training scheme. The scheme details specific

standards which employees work towards. During his on-the-job training Alan has the opportunity of working towards the Silver Badge level, the Technical Skills level and the Team Expert level.

Diane accesses her future
In the earlier days of being at home, Diane did take an access course in order to prepare herself for entry into university. Because the course was part-time she could rest her back in between. Upon completion of the access course Diane was offered a university place, but it proved too much strain for her back. Now she is aware that any study needs to be done at home, hence her French and book-keeping study. She is also considering an OU course.

Tony takes a byte
Tony is considering a further education course in computer-aided engineering, as computers are something of a hobby for him, and he could combine an interest with an engineering background.

Mel wants to go it alone
Mel has decided she wants to work for herself. That way she can have as much responsibility as she likes and the sky's her limit for earning. She would like to develop her administration and management skills. She also needs to learn how to run her own business. She is applying to the TEC (Training and Enterprise Council) to see if they offer courses to business people. She is also checking out the courses at her local college and with open colleges.

DISCUSSION POINTS

1. Do you think that learning interpersonal skills for the workplace should be a crucial part of the national curriculum?

2. What are the main differences in taking a further education course and a higher education course, in terms of influencing career decisions?

3. Which NVQs are relevant to your trade or profession?

4
Paying for the Training

CONSIDERING YOUR FINANCIAL OBLIGATIONS

When considering which course to take, you will need to review your financial situation. Domestic obligations would include:

- rent or mortgage
- council tax
- water rates
- electricity and gas
- telephone
- insurances
- food
- dependants
- leisure
- clothing.

Specific costs relevant to your course might include:

- course fees
- extra course materials, *eg* books
- transport to and from your course
- childcare
- exam fees.

FINDING SOURCES OF FUNDING

Using the local education authorities (LEA)
LEAs publish booklets containing information on mandatory and discretionary grants, plus other forms of assistance available to students.
 Discretionary awards are often made if you:

– are a part-time student
– are studying with the Open University

- are on an access course
- have been accepted on to a part-time foundation course for a degree.

Training and enterprise council (TEC)
Some funding for access courses may be obtainable through the above council.

Obtaining financial assistance for medical work
The Department of Health administers discretionary awards for occupational therapy, orthoptics, dental therapy, radiography, physiotherapy and dental hygiene.

Students considering nursing may obtain assistance through the **Project 2000** diploma courses.

Applying to the Department for Education and Employment
Student Grants and Loans: a brief guide for higher education students is available from the careers service or the Department for Education and Employment.

If you are considering a two-year residential course leading to a diploma, which fulfils the criteria leading to higher education, you could apply for a state bursary which covers fees, board and a personal allowance.

Going to the students' union
Most universities and colleges have a students' union which can advise on sources of funding.

Finding out about mandatory grants
If you have been resident in the UK for three years prior to the start of the academic year your course is due to start in, you may be entitled to a **mandatory award** or **grant**. The grant consists of two parts: the **tuition fees**, and the **maintenance grant** which is means-tested. The grant covers a first degree, a Postgraduate Certificate in Education, a Higher National Diploma and a Diploma of Higher Education.

If you have been accepted on a full-time foundation course for a degree you may be entitled to a mandatory award.

Getting the fees waived by colleges
If you are claiming benefits, some colleges waive the fees (make sure the course is less than sixteen hours in length) and charge only a minimal enrolment fee.

Exploring allowances

Mature Student's Allowance
If you are over 25 years of age and have had a total income of more than £12,000 gross in the three years prior to entering higher education, you may be entitled to the **Mature Student's Allowance**.

Dependants Allowance
If you have a partner who does not have an income, you may be entitled to the **Dependants Allowance**. You may also be entitled to the allowance if you have children for whom you are responsible. If you are disabled you may be eligible for extra allowances.

Access funds
Further and higher education operate access funds. They are available if you are over 19 and live in the UK. Criteria vary from institution to institution, with unemployed single parents having priority.

Applying to charities
Your local reference library will have a register of charities which are prepared to help mature students. Examples include *The Grants Register* (Macmillan) and the *Education Grants Directory* (Directory of Social Change).

Using your redundancy money
If you have been made redundant, and have received a financial package, you might consider investing some of the money in your future via training.

Getting company sponsorship
Many companies look for students to invest in. Students are usually required to sign a contract with the company, which requires them to undergo training with the company during the academic year and to work for them for around six to ten weeks during the summer holiday. In return, the student receives an allowance, which is paid on top of the grant, and is paid a salary for the time he/she works during the holidays. Companies advertise their sponsorship package in careers service offices or through *The Which Guide to Sponsorships in Higher Education* (Consumers Association).

Taking advantage of in-house training
If you are in work your company may offer courses and workshops for staff development purposes, which wouldn't cost you a penny.

Obtaining free training when unemployed
The **Jobseeker's Allowance** (JSA) is the new benefit for unemployed people which will replace the two existing benefits: Unemployment Benefit and Income Support. Speak to your claimant adviser prior to starting any course to make sure your benefit is protected.

Training for Work
Training for Work is a major programme for long-term unemployed adults to return to the labour market. Training and Enterprise Councils (TECs) are responsible for operating these programmes locally. Training for Work was introduced in 1993 'to help long-term unemployed persons... get jobs through training and work experience'.

A typical participant's programme may include:

- job-specific training
- working towards a National Vocational Qualification
- work experience.

Examples of the types of NVQ on a Training for Work scheme might include Business Administration, Accounting, Warehousing, IT and Care. In order to join a Training for Work programme you:

- need to be aged between 18 – 63

- need to have been continuously unemployed for at least twenty-six weeks

- may be endorsed by Employment Services with a disability and are unemployed (not necessarily for twenty-six weeks)

- may be an unemployed (not necessarily for twenty-six weeks) person whose numeracy or literacy difficulties impairs their chances of employment

- may be an unemployed (not necessarily for twenty-six weeks) person for whom English is not their first language, thereby making employment opportunities limited

- may be an unemployed ex-offender with at least twenty-six continuous weeks qualifying time made up of time spent in custody, on remand or on a supervision order

- may be an ex-regular who, for the qualifying twenty-six weeks of unemployment, have been in HM Armed Services

- have been the victim of a 'large-scale redundancy' and have since been continuously unemployed for a period not exceeding twenty-six weeks

- are a lone parent who has been unemployed for at least twenty-six weeks

- are a returner to the labour market

- are not an overseas national

- are not on a government-funded business start-up scheme

- are not on a modern apprenticeship

- are not on Workstart

- are not on Work Trial

- are not on YT.

You can join a Training for Work programme directly, by approaching a TEC provider. In most cases you are likely to be referred by an Employment Service adviser. When you join one of these programmes you will still continue to receive JSA plus a weekly premium of £10.

Lone parents entering a Training for Work Programme can be given assistance with the costs of caring for their children.

Youth Credits
These are designed to help young people buy their own training. Access to Youth Training and Modern Apprenticeships are through these credits. Under this programme young people leaving school are given a **voucher** or **credit**, which enables them to buy training from approved providers such as colleges or employers. Once the young person is in training, the providers redeem the credit for cash from the local TEC.

Part-time study
In order to safeguard your JSA you need to be classed as a part-time student. If you are considering taking an adult or further education vocational course, and as long as you're taking a course of not more than sixteen tutor-led learning hours (but up to twenty-one hours with home study) per week, you are a part-time student. If you are considering higher education, your course provider will need to produce evidence for Employment Service purposes that the course is not full-time.

When you feel ready to take a part-time course, you need to inform your claimant adviser who will give you a questionnaire to complete. This will assess whether your participation on a course will affect your entitlement to JSA.

There is a provision for those wanting to take an employment-related, short full-time course, lasting no longer than two weeks without this affecting their JSA.

Access courses are classified as part-time study.

OBTAINING WELFARE BENEFITS

Housing
If you are a lone parent, disabled or living with a partner who doesn't have an income, have children or are living on a pension, you may be eligible for housing benefit.

In-work benefits
If you are on a low salary it is possible to qualify for in-work benefits which would top up your income. Individual calculation is done by a claimant adviser at your local Jobcentre.

Other benefit entitlements
Additional benefits you may be entitled to include maternity allowance, income support or unemployment benefit.

Advice agencies
The Citizens Advice Bureau or local authority welfare benefits unit may help.

Eligibility
If you are claiming benefits you can study for up to sixteen hours per week without your benefits being affected.

GETTING A LOAN

The Students Loans Company is an organisation specifically set up to help students under 50 through university or college.

Career Development Loans

With this type of loan the individual will normally have to pay at least twenty per cent of the course fees. If you have been unemployed for three months or longer, you may be able to borrow one hundred per cent. You will be responsible for the repayment of the loan, although you don't have to make any repayments during the period of the course and for one month following completion (or six months if you remain unemployed). Points to bear in mind include:

1. You can apply for up to eighty per cent of course fees, plus the full cost of books and other support material.
2. If the course is full-time you can apply for living expenses.
3. You can borrow between £200 – £8,000.
4. The period of training supported cost-wise must not be longer than two years, although the course itself may be longer.
5. You may be able to get assistance with travel costs.
6. Child-minding fees may also be included.
7. You must live or intend to train in Great Britain.
8. None of the costs you request to be covered can be paid for from any other source.
9. The course mustn't attract a mandatory or full discretionary award.
10. The course you apply for must be vocational (work-related). It can be part- or full-time, college or university, attended or distance or open learning.

Career Development Loans are obtained through four banks:

- Royal Bank of Scotland
- Co-operative
- Barclays
- Clydesdale.

Loans and JSA
Check with your claimant adviser at the Jobcentre as to how a Career Development Loan may affect your JSA.

CASE STUDIES

Alan's company pays the bill
Alan's company is paying for his training. On-the-job training is becoming more popular because employers don't have to lose their workers for the length of the course.

Diane pays as she goes
Diane is having private tuition with a qualified tutor and is paying on a weekly basis.

Tony is negotiating
The further education course Tony is interested in would benefit the telecommunication company he is currently working for. Although he intends leaving at some point in the future, Tony would use his new skills where he is working now, so he has negotiated that the company pays half the course fees and he pays the other half.

Mel spreads the cost
Mel has discovered that her local Enterprise Agency is offering free one-day seminars to people setting up their own businesses. The management studies skills course she is considering doing through a reputable open college will accept staggered payments.

DISCUSSION POINTS

1. If you are a mature student returning to study, how would you feel if the financial obligations fell on your partner?

2. If you are working, explore the training opportunities in your company. Would your company pay to send you on a course? Is on-the-job training available to you? How might you improve your skills and knowledge?

3. If you are unemployed, what Training for Work opportunities are there in your area which might interest you?

5
Coping as an Adult Student

There might be any number of reasons why you wish to return to education or training. Consider:

☐ Do you need stimulus in your life?
☐ Do you want to follow an interest in depth over a long period of time?
☐ Do you want to obtain a qualification to enter a specific career?
☐ Do you want to look for a new direction in your life?
☐ Do you want to progress in your existing career?
☐ Do you want to prove yourself?

It is important at the outset to consider the *reasons* for wanting to learn. The more powerful your motivations, the more chance you have of succeeding.

Once you have decided on your motivations – money, recognition or status – you then need to prepare the ground of your consciousness with regard to how you see yourself fitting in with college and university life.

OVERCOMING PRECONCEPTIONS ABOUT OTHER STUDENTS

As adults we often have an image of students. We tend primarily to think of them as young. How we build up our internal picture from there might vary.

How do you perceive the 'traditional' student?

wearing scruffy clothes	staying up all night	pleading poverty
drunk	drug-taking	left-wing
earnest and bespectacled	driving a 2-CV	riding a pedal bike

The reality is that many students are now mature learners. They often account for at least a quarter in any institution, even half in some. Because of the change in working trends, many adults are choosing to change career direction or, in some cases, to return to work after bringing up a family. There is an increase in women returning to study, not only to enhance their career prospects but to express themselves away from their work and family.

Learning with young people

It is natural, although incorrect, to assume that younger students are academically superior to adults. Young people may be quicker, but adult learners bring maturity, life experience, wisdom and reliability to college and university life.

BALANCING HOME AND STUDY

There are likely to be more demands on your time with regard to family and social commitments. Housework and domestic rotas may have to be reorganised. You might need to consider where you will study when at home.

Managing family commitments

Studying is likely to affect the time you have with your family. The time may increase or decrease due to the restructuring of your timetable. Hopefully you will have more quality time with your family.

If dependants are affecting your choice of course, you might need to consider open or distance learning. If you have children, check if the college or university has crèche facilities. You also need to consider school holidays. With regard to children and other dependants, ask your tutor:

- Can you have tutorials over the phone?
- How many workshops/seminars/lectures do you have to attend?
- How much study are you expected to put in away from the classroom?

Questions to ask yourself
- How will I cope with childcare when I need to go into college or university?
- How will my partner react to my becoming a student?
- How do I feel about the label 'student'?
- Am I self-motivated enough to study?
- Do I mind spending time reading?

Coping as an Adult Student

- How would I feel about spending time largely with people younger than myself?
- How good am I at organising my own timetable?

Travelling time
Travel can take up a large amount of time. When choosing your course and university ask yourself:

1. Could I live on campus during term-time?
2. Could I commute to campus from home?
3. How far am I willing to travel daily? What is the cost?

Time management
As an adult learner, you need to organise and manage your time effectively for maximum impact. Consider the following:

sleeping	eating	personal hygiene
shopping	looking after pets	looking after children
looking after dependants	housework	time with friends
	travelling	gardening
watching TV	hobbies	listening to the radio
cooking	home DIY/	paying bills/paperwork
fitness/sport	maintenance	time with your partner

Is there anything else you might spend time doing? Now draw a circle and allocate chunks of time for all the activities which you might do in one day. Do the same exercise again, but let the circle represent one week.

Ask yourself:

1. What are the proportions of time I spend on each activity?
2. Am I spending time doing something which I can delegate to someone else?
3. What can I let go of?
4. How can I reorganise my schedule to fit in study hours?

Earning while you're learning
As an adult your living circumstances are likely to be particular to *you*. You might consider going back to live with your parents. Your partner may have an income which can support you both (or the

MY NETWORKING WEB

My domestic network contacts:...

My health network contacts:...

My transport network contacts:..

My family network contacts: ....

My social network contacts: ....

My interest and hobby network contacts: ....

My educational network contacts:.......................................

My personal support network contacts: ....

My spiritual network contacts: ....

Fig. 7. Developing a networking web.

family), you might live on your own or with friends. You might be retired. You may be doing paid work. Ask yourself:

1. What alterations might I have to make to my lifestyle?
2. Do I need to organise another source of income?
3. How much do I need to support myself or contribute to the family income?
4. Have I found out everything about benefits I might be entitled to?

Sources of financial information
These include Citizens Advice Bureaux, Jobcentres, welfare rights centres, student centres with colleges and universities, and the library.

GETTING SUPPORT

Special needs
Students with physical or mental disabilities are frequently given additional support within universities and colleges. If you find that their practice does not always match up to their verbal commitment, say something and ask for the support you are entitled to.

Student services
Most colleges and universities have a health centre, counselling services, a students' union, a welfare centre and may even have facilities for worship.

Building a support network
It is important that you build up your own network of tutorial and personal support. See Figure 7 for details of the kinds of networks you may need.

Your social network at college of university
Life isn't all about study at college or university. There is entertainment, sport and recreation, shops, bars and cafés specifically geared towards the student.

INCREASING YOUR CONFIDENCE

Many mature would-be students feel they are not qualified for acceptance onto a course because they lack confidence. Older

SKILLS A MATURE STUDENT HAS TO OFFER

Define your skills as all the practical things you have learnt to do

- providing first-aid
- budgeting
- managing your time
- supervising others
- supporting in crisis
- counselling
- route-planning
- doing clerical work
- diagnosing
- improvising
- making things
- performing
- promoting change
- researching
- working with words
- organisation recreational activities
- using a home computer
- setting priorities
- motivating others
- finding sources of information
- driving
- administration
- designing
- dissecting information
- leading
- organising
- problem-solving
- repairing
- using machines

Fig. 8. Assessing a mature student's skills.

students tend to undervalue their past work experience, paid or unpaid, and their role in bringing up a family. Mature learners bring many skills and strengths into college and university by the value of their experience.

Confidence is about having belief in yourself and your abilities. Comparing yourself to other people, old or young, won't help your sense of self-esteem. You need to be aware of your own skills and strengths, how you have learnt them and what you are doing with them now. *Who you are now* and *what you hope to aspire to* are the important factors. By reading this book, you are considering improving your work prospects by taking up some form of education or training. This shows you are curious and seeking to better yourself. Good for you. The fact that you are thinking of going to college or university indicates you are considering a change, partial or total, in life-style. You're a risk-taker as well.

Young people at college or university may have several factors in their favour but, as a mature learner, so have you. Being older doesn't mean clapped out and on the scrapheap. It means gaining knowledge and life experience and being able to transfer those across to the learning environment. Why not learn from young people? They will want to learn from you. After all – you are already where they are going.

Further skills
Mature students also bring the following skills to the learning place.

Problem-solving
– Defining the situation through information gathering.
– Having realistic goals.
– Making realistic predictions.
– Monitoring the implementation of a plan.
– Evaluating a plan.

Decision-making
How do you make decisions?
– Logically and objectively.
– Morally and ethically.
– Impulsively.
– By delaying through procrastination.
– Via feeling and intuition.
– Passively, according to the expectations of others.
– By getting too involved with detail and the assessment process.

STRENGTHS A MATURE STUDENT HAS TO OFFER
Define your strengths as your personal qualities

- adaptable
- ambitious
- cautious
- competitive
- decisive
- emotional
- gentle
- imaginative
- introspective
- objective
- outgoing
- persistent
- resilient
- sensitive to others
- adventurous
- assertive
- changeable
- confident
- dependable
- energetic
- hard-working
- independent
- just
- obstinate
- passive
- positive
- resourceful
- stable

- aggressive
- capable
- cheerful
- consistent
- easy-going
- excitable
- helpful
- innovative
- loyal
- open-minded
- people-pleaser
- reliable
- security minded
- tactful
- aloof
- caring
- cooperative
- daring
- efficient
- forceful
- humorous
- intellectual
- methodical
- organised
- perfectionist
- reserved
- self-reliant
- trustworthy

Fig. 9. Assessing a mature student's strengths.

Friends and family may perceive you as different – more intelligent. Your children may feel an alliance with you for 'going to school'.

Mature students in higher education tend to find they change and develop, not only academically, but personally. Students become more self-confident, and assertive, more logical and increase in self-respect.

USING THE UNIVERSITY OF THE THIRD AGE

More people approaching or entering retirement are considering a 'third-age career'. There is a growing number of mature students who are in their 50s. The University of the Third Age has over two hundred centres throughout the country offering courses specifically for the more mature. Many are linked to colleges.

University of the Third Age, 1 Stockwell Green, London SW9 9JF.

MAKING EXPERIENCE COUNT

I have been working with adult students for the past fifteen years. At the age of 28 I became a part-time mature student. I'm now 38 and I'm sure I haven't stopped learning yet.

Calling on my experience as a tutor and trainer, I find working with adults rewarding. There is much give and take of knowledge and skills. A good tutor will always encourage the adults in their group to contribute their experience, and to help guide more vulnerable and younger students.

There can be problems when training adults inasmuch as their personal life can sometimes intrude, *eg* childcare, health problems or family breakups. However, these are practicalities which can be overcome, as long as the basic motivation for learning is there.

One last thing while speaking as a trainer. There have been off days for me, when I have lacked confidence or have been feeling negative or uptight about something in my personal life. I have always found mature students to be patient and understanding, which are qualities of value.

CASE STUDIES

Alan is paid to learn

Alan is a young man in his 20s. He has chosen to work in the leisure industry, specialising in food and drink. His motivation is to be in a social environment with young people. His on-the-job training happens in his chosen social context, where he is also getting paid, and is very different from the school he remembers.

Diane guides others

When Diane took the access course she was one of the more mature students. She enjoyed this role because it brought out the mother in her. Others sought her opinion and this made her feel more confident. Now she is working on a one-to-one basis with a tutor who is older than herself.

Tony finds companions

Tony is one of the older students on his computer course. Even so, most of the other students are in their late 20s and 30s and most are men. Several of them share similar experiences, such as family life or wanting to change career direction. He can attend his course in the evening.

Mel finds she has taken on a lot

Mel has started her management studies course by correspondence. Because she wants to start her own business she is disciplined and motivated to work on her own. She does have contact with her tutor by phone and post, and there are some weekend seminars to attend where she will meet like-minded people. She is finding it hard to fit study in alongside a full-time job.

DISCUSSION POINTS

1. Analyse your preconceived ideas about college or university life. On what do you base your ideas?

2. According to your own value system, how should a mature student behave?

3. What are the benefits of learning in later life?

6
Keeping Up with the Course

REMEMBERING HOW YOU'VE LEARNED

When we were young and in formal education, we may have had limited choice over subject matter. Consequently our motivations could have been low. We may not have been good at a subject or we may have not liked a particular teacher. Many adults have negative memories of their schooldays and returning to study or education can seem daunting. However, as adults we have choice and freedom. We can set our own goals and work out strategies for achieving them. Consider two learning experiences you have had as an adult (formal or informal) and analyse them from a negative and a successful perspective.

	NEGATIVE EXPERIENCE	SUCCESSFUL EXPERIENCE
Were you interested in the subject?		
Could you relate to the teaching?		
What kind of tutorial help did you have?		
Could you apply your learning?		
What do you remember most?		

Most people need:

- to be motivated if the learning is to be effective

- time to take new learning in before moving on

- to see their learning applied on a personal level

- to have support from tutors and from other students.

WHAT IS YOUR LEARNING STYLE?

Do you:

Need a challenge?	......
Need a good reason for taking a course?	......
Like to have things organised?	......
Prefer detailed instruction?	......
Like to try things on your own?	......
Read around a subject area?	......
Keep yourself motivated?	......
Like to work methodically?	......
Prefer tutors telling you what to do?	......
Enjoy learning by doing?	......
Like your progress to be checked as you go along?	......
Need to be regularly prodded into action?	......
Prefer to negotiate what you will do with your tutors?	......
Like to do one thing at a time?	......
Like to have several things on the go at once?	......
Like to work with others?	......
Think exams and tests are an accurate reflection of your progress?	......
Need the discipline of a timetable?	......

Fig. 10. Finding what way of learning suits you.

Keeping Up with the Course

Learning in the best way
There are many different ways we can learn something new. In every case, we need a facilitator or tutor to guide us. But the methods the facilitator or tutor uses will affect the way in which we learn. (See Figure 10.)

LOOKING AT YOUR MOTIVATIONS

Why do you want to learn:

- To get a higher salary?
- To obtain a more interesting job?
- To get a piece of paper?
- To do something you've always wanted to do?
- To increase your confidence?
- To impress somebody?

Setting goals
If we are to study effectively, we need to set goals. Good goals should be:

S	M	A	R	T
p	a	c	e	i
e	n	h	a	m
c	a	i	l	e
i	g	e	i	b
f	e	v	s	o
i	a	a	t	u
c	b	b	i	n
	l	l	c	d
	e	e		

Check that your study goals take into account holidays, paid work, family commitments and social activities. Could you cope if something unexpected, such as illness, happened?

Planning your time
You will need to draw up a timetable based on a reasonable allocation of available time, allowing time for revision and consolidation. Family commitments and social life need to be taken into account. Try to set aside a period for reading each day, ideally taking key notes at the same time.

Make a timetable for yourself, not forgetting to build in relaxation and pleasant rewards. When timetabling study periods, make sure you choose the times of the day where you feel mentally alert.

BUILDING CONCENTRATION

What stops you from concentrating on study?

- the telephone
- the TV
- family or friends asking questions
- the children
- hunger
- tiredness
- boredom
- heat and cold
- illness.

What else stops *you* from concentrating?

If interruptions are a problem, maybe you need to have a specific area of the house for study where *no one* interrupts you. Maybe you could consider the library.

Making the learning relevant to you

One of the best ways we learn is when we see the relevance of something new as an extension of what we already know. I've given below the example of taking an NVQ in Business Administration. At present I have a good basic knowledge of office procedure, which I use to run my business. If I were considering taking the Business Admin NVQ 3 I would need to see the relevance to my working future. I would also feel better if I was extending my existing knowledge (confidence booster). The section on how the learning might improve my career prospects would provide the motivation for taking the NVQ.

What do I already know?
telephone skills
basic computer stationery
opening and sorting mail
basic filing
setting out business letters
dealing with new people
managing my own schedule
ordering office stationery
sending out invoices
replying to letters
word processing
operating a fax
organising travel
attending meetings

How do I use the knowledge and skills?
To run my business as a freelance trainer.

What new things might I learn from Business Admin NVQ Level 3?

sending mail overseas
advanced word processing skills
resourcing public documents
increased use of computer graphics
organising the binding of documents

sending e-mail
use of databases
research skills
organising business visits
keeping a petty cash system
monitoring health and safety

How might this learning improve my career prospects?
Improve my efficiency in running a business.
Develop into becoming an NVQ assessor for Business Administration.

| EFFECTIVE LEARNING | = | ACTIVE LEARNING |

Active learning is about questioning what, who, when, how, where and why?

SOLVING PROBLEMS

Problem-solving is one of the major keys to effective study. The seven steps to effective problem-solving are to:

1. Identify the problem.
2. Analyse the problem.
3. Obtain information.
4. Consider alternative solutions.
5. Weigh up the advantages and disadvantages of the proposed solutions.
6. Take action.
7. Evaluate the results.

Reading skills
We read for pleasure, to obtain information, to understand something, to find an answer to a question or to gain more information.
There are four main techniques we use when reading:

1. **Word by word**. Exam papers, for example.
2. **Skimming**. When we think of borrowing or buying a book we skim the contents and introduction.
3. **Focused reading**. Such as detailed study of a chapter or chunk of text.
4. **Scanning**. A focused overview of a chapter to search for a particular detail, for instance.

Using textbooks
Effective methods of reading include:

- **Active reading** from a textbook using the 3R method – read, recite, record.

- **Robinson's SQ3r method**: survey, question, read, recite, review.

- **Pauk's OK5R method**: overview, key ideas, read, record, recite, review, reflect.

The marking of your own textbooks to assist in memorising is a good learning aid. Read sections or paragraphs fully before underlining and use symbols in consistent fashion to mark matter requiring further study.

Remembering what you've learnt
Recital, **review** and **practice** in retrieval contribute to long-term remembering. Seek associations within the subject area:

Verbal
- Group things together.
- Pair things together.
- Link with things you already know.
- Make up a story linking things together.

Visual
- Group things together and visualise them.
- Write a list and visualise it.

Repetition
- Write out a number of times.
- Repeat aloud a number of times.
- Read over and over again.

Conditions for good recall
- There is a tendency to remember the last thing you read.
- The more you test yourself the more you learn.
- The more you concentrate the more you learn.
- The more important the material is to you, the more you learn.
- Your state of mind affects what you learn.
- The more you can relate the material to be learned to other things, the more you learn.

Taking notes

Why
For reference, revision, to restructure meaning, as an aide-mémoire, to register concentration/clarity.

Where
In notebooks, binders, on cards, in an index or file.

When
After reading, while reading, during or after lecture/radio/TV.

How
Type, write, use standard or personal abbreviation, use logical layout, use colour, diagrams, sentences, symbols, headings, underlining, numbering.

What
Main ideas, key words, essential details, sources, references.

Improving your writing skills

During your study you may need to write:

- assignments
- reports
- letters
- essays
- projects
- summaries
- notes

Writing skills checklist

1. How long should the piece of writing be?

2. Should you use double or single spacing?

3. Should you use headings?
4. Can you include other people's ideas from your reading?
5. Can you write on one or both sides of the paper?
6. Should you include your own ideas?
7. Should you word process the documents or can you handwrite it?
8. Should you include evidence of your own research?
9. Should you write in paragraph or note form?
10. Can you include illustrations?

Learning word processing
It is an idea, if your course contains a lot of writing, to learn word processing. When you use a word processor, you can input and save long documents and retrieve them at a later date to alter them.

Further education and adult education offer courses, or you could enrol on an intensive course with a private secretarial school. You may even be able to use the IT equipment on campus.

Getting support
How you approach your learning experience, and what you gain from it, will be affected by the amount of support you ask for. Consider the following:

- Use your tutor as a resource.
- If in doubt – ask.
- Use your peers.
- Improve your learning skills.
- Improve your study skills.

Studying and learning, especially as an adult, should be a pleasure. The majority of a learning experience should be positive and relevant to your working future.

Whether a young person or a mature adult, stay connected to *why* you want to take a course, and as long as those reasons are truly *what you want*, you can overcome any challenges which surround study skills. Study skills can be learnt. Your motivation and reasons for learning are already within you.

CASE STUDIES

Alan wants to be treated like an adult
Alan remembers what he wants to. If it is fun and something he can try for himself, he is more receptive. His memories of school aren't far away, so he responds better if he is taught adult-to-adult rather than adult-to-teenager. His motivations at the moment are money and status.

Diane needs a challenge
Since Diane's accident she doesn't feel as if she is contributing either to the household finances (she's married and her husband works) or to being of service to others. She also needs taking out of herself and to focus on things other than her health. Her mind is quick and receptive, and she sees any problems with her learning as challenges to be overcome.

Tony wants out
Tony is under stress with his work and has to work under pressure. Because he is something of a perfectionist, he was anxious when he started his computer course at college, but now he is seeing it as a way out of his current work situation and this is acting as a spur. He is able to use some of his learning in his daily work, which helps him to learn more quickly.

Mel is struggling
Mel is hungry to have more responsibility and run her own business. In some ways she is taking on too much and trying too hard, but she is aware of this problem and is reorganising her timetable.

DISCUSSION POINTS

1. Consider your favourite subject at school. How were you taught?

2. Discuss the following: 'Tell me and I forget, show me and I may remember, involve me and I'll understand.'

3. What was your motivation for reading this book?

7
Gaining a Qualification while Staying at Home

You may be in a situation where the attendance of college or university presents barriers which are difficult to overcome. You may:

- be bringing up a family
- be a carer
- have a disability
- live in a remote area which makes travelling into a learning institute difficult.

If you are highly motivated to learn new job skills, but cannot attend a college or university, then open or distance learning is just right for you.

DEFINING OPEN LEARNING

Open learning is a term used to define methods of learning which allow the learner to take charge of their programme of study. The student works at a time, place and pace suited to them. In order to do this learners require a wide variety of material designed to take the tutor's place, providing specially prepared information and exercises. To support this learning students should have access to a tutor, via post, phone or tutorial meetings, and to the choice of meeting with other students, (such as summer schools and drop-in study centres).

Benefits of open learning

Open or **distance learning** is a very flexible way of gaining qualifications for the following reasons:

- You can design your learning around your lifestyle.

- You can normally start a course when you like, not just at the start of an academic year.

Gaining a Qualification while Staying at Home

- You can pace the learning to suit yourself.
- There is a huge choice of courses available.

CHOOSING A COURSE

When choosing a course you need to ask yourself:

1. Is the qualification widely recognised in the workplace?
2. What kind of facilities does the open learning centre/unit have?
3. By the end of the course do I get a full or part qualification?
4. Do I have complete access to all of the facilities available?
5. Will I be assessed by exam or continuous assessment?
6. Are there any hidden financial extras in connection with the facilities?
7. Will I meet other students?
8. Is there a summer school?
9. What kind of tutorial support is there?
10. Is there a time limit for completion of the course?

OPEN COLLEGES

An open (or correspondence) college requires self-discipline. The courses they offer usually result in a qualification, while the **packages** are designed for retraining or updating skills.

Council for the Accreditation of Correspondence Colleges (CACC)

This body exists to develop a system of accreditation approved by the Department for Education and Employment. It is an independent body which inspects every aspect of a college and gives approval if the Council's criteria are met.

Most open colleges are private companies. Unless a college has been accredited by the CACC, you need to ask:

- Can they send you an example of specimen material?
- When were the course notes last revised?
- Do they give refunds?
- How much tutor support is there? How is this support given?
- Are the tutors qualified?
- How is the student assessed?
- What is the qualification offered and by whom is that accredited?

National Extension College
This open college offers a wide range of educational services, including:

- open learning resources
- distance learning courses with full tutor support
- training materials
- staff development programmes.

Their vocational training includes NVQs in administration, accounting, care and IT. Other training includes voluntary and community work, office skills, essential business skills, information design and marketing.

Other courses include counselling, caring and health, teaching and training, and basic and general education.

Taking an Open University course
This university requires no entry qualification (except for higher degrees). You can fit in your studies around the rest of your life, and seventy-five per cent of OU students remain in full-time employment throughout their studies. Many students are sponsored by their employers.

Students on OU courses receive personal attention and support from their network of tutors. There are opportunities to meet them and your fellow students in tutorials, self-help groups and residential schools. The university actively encourages mature students, and more than 165,000 students of all ages and backgrounds have obtained OU degrees.

Points about OU courses
- You have the option of spreading your study over several years, with breaks.

- Most students are part-time.

- Degree courses contain a mixture of course units, notes, exercises, self-assessment tests, assignments, audio tapes, records, slides, videos, broadcasts, options to attend study centres and summer schools.

- Non-degree courses are offered.

- The academic year runs from February to November.

- Most learning is done through correspondence, radio, TV, audio-visual materials, workbooks and personal tutor contact.

- There is the option of self-standing materials.

STUDYING AT HOME

While studying at home has plenty of benefits, it also brings new challenges.

Finding a place to study
You will need to ensure you have a place to study. Will you use the kitchen or lounge table? Will you put your books away after each use or can you leave them out? Will sticky little fingers explore through your valuable resources?

Ideally a specific room, away from family bustle and people making requests, would be good, but if that isn't possible try to make a special place in the home for your study.

Working around the family
You will need to make boundaries when you want to study. Requests from family and friends will have to take second place. Getting into the habit of time management and timetabling should help.

Equally you need quality time, both with your family – especially if you are a carer – and with yourself. Explain to your family at the start what you are trying to do and why it is so important to you. Ask their cooperation so that they feel part of what is going on.

Getting disciplined
There will be times when you will want to sit out in the garden, go out for that drink, eat something or watch TV. Maybe it would be good for you to give in. All study and no play makes Jack and Jill boring people and prone to burn-out. However, there will be many times when you will have to be firm with yourself, ignore all temptations and get on with your study. At times like this set yourself targets with a reward at the end.

Keeping yourself motivated
Always keep in mind *why* you are studying. Remember what it is

that you're trying to achieve. You're taking this course to get a better job, to improve your confidence, to make more money, to get promotion, to return to work; but most of all you are doing it because it is the *right thing for you* and it makes you feel good about yourself.

CASE STUDIES

Alan is earning and learning
Alan learns best on the job. He isn't often at home enough to study! If he's not working, he's out with his friends.

Diane studies in comfort
As Diane is unable to get to university to take advantage of her place, she is considering doing an OU course.

Tony works on his home computer
Tony has a computer at home. It was this interest which sparked off the idea of doing computer-aided engineering. He completes his written work at home and is developing an interest in teaching himself programming.

Mel is building her future
As Mel is doing a distance learning course, she fits in her studies at home around her working life.

DISCUSSION POINTS

1. Analyse the pros and cons of taking a course which you study from home.

2. More companies are encouraging their staff to take a course which involves study at home. Would you consider doing this?

3. Research the open learning centres local to you, including the library. What might you do that would be useful to your career progression?

8
Gaining a Qualification and Working Full-Time

It is possible to gain a qualification, specifically a National Vocational Qualification (NVQ), based on what you do in your own working environment.

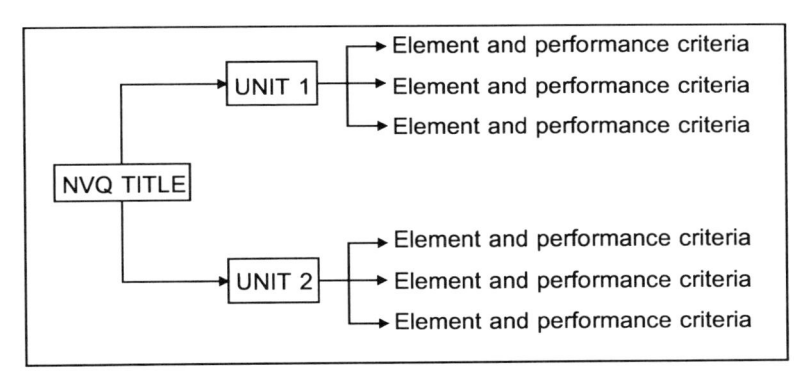

```
NVQ TITLE ──┬── UNIT 1 ──┬── Element and performance criteria
            │            ├── Element and performance criteria
            │            └── Element and performance criteria
            │
            └── UNIT 2 ──┬── Element and performance criteria
                         ├── Element and performance criteria
                         └── Element and performance criteria
```

Fig. 11. The NVQ structure.

EXPLAINING THE NVQ SYSTEM

NVQs are offered at five different levels and indicate that a person is able (**competent**) to perform a specific range of work-related tasks. NVQs are associated with particular occupations and are broken down into units. These units may have an application in more than one occupational sector. Because the NVQ system is unit based the candidate can build up **credits** for part-completion of an NVQ.

Flexibility
With NVQs there is flexibility of:

- learning approaches
- length of time taken to complete
- location of learning (the candidate's place of work is the most common place).

Some of the wide range of available NVQs

accounting	administration	agriculture
aircraft maintenance	animal care	aquatics
banking	beauty therapy	boat building
book editing	book publishing	broadcast and film
building site management	bus and coach driving	business administration
business counselling	care	catering and hospitality
child care and education	construction	craft baking
demolition	design	dry cleaning
engineering	fish husbandry	floristry
footwear repair	forestry	horse care
horticulture	housing management	insurance
licensed bookmaking	newspaper journalism	photography
postnatal care	press photography	racehorse care
sea fishing	security guarding	shopfitting
software production	sports coaching	steeplejacking

Fig. 12. NVQs on offer.

The importance of assessment
Successful completion is through **continuous assessment**. It is impossible to fail an NVQ because if you, the candidate, don't come through a particular assessment by providing evidence of your competence you just practise until you get it right, then get assessed again until you have the right evidence to match the criteria. A candidate is either competent or not competent.

You don't have to take all of an NVQ at once. You can build up credits towards an NVQ and these will be recorded. Units can be gained gradually.

Setting the standards
A number of bodies are responsible for setting and monitoring the NVQ standards.

National Council for Vocational Qualifications (NCVQ)
This body defines the criteria against which qualifications are measured for accreditation and gives the qualifications a level within the NVQ framework. They ensure that quality management is practised and accredit qualifications with the NVQ standard.

Awarding bodies
These bodies include names such as City and Guilds, RSA and BTEC who are responsible for the assessment and certification of NVQs. They work closely with other organisations such as the **lead bodies** and submit the qualifications to NCVQ for accreditation.

Lead bodies
Lead bodies represent specific occupations. They may be industry training organisations such as the Hotel and Catering Company or a consortia of various occupational representatives such as the National Retail Training Council. The lead body identifies the standards of competence relevant to their occupational sector, and packages the standards into qualifications which meet the requirements of the occupational sector and also the NCVQ's accreditation criteria.

The lead bodies liaise with **awarding bodies** on assessment, and may also involve themselves directly in the assessment and certification process.

Understanding the structure
An NVQ is arranged in **units** and **elements**. Whole units can be

NVQ/SVQ level	Description	GNVQ/GSVQ level	Relevant to
Level 1	Foundation	Foundation	4 GCSEs at Grades D-G. National Curriculum levels 5/6. National Certificate (level I)
Level 2	Basic craft	Intermediate	4-5 GCSE grades A-C/SCE Standard grades. National Curriculum level 7, National Certificate (level II)
Level 3	Technician Advanced Craft Supervisor	Advanced	2+ GCE A-Levels or equivalent in AS/SCE Higher Grades and Certificates of Sixth Year Studies National Certificate (level III)
Level 4	Higher Technician Junior Management		Higher Education (HND/HNC)
Level 5	Professional Middle Management		Higher Education (Degree)

Fig. 13. NVQ relevance to other qualifications.
(Adapted from *Getting into Vocational Qualifications* [Trotman].)

Gaining a Qualification and Working Full-Time

taken without actually taking an entire NVQ. I am an NVQ assessor and have taken two units, D32 and D33, which are only part of a large NVQ to do with training and development. Each unit is then broken down into elements which set out specific criteria a candidate has to meet, and to provide evidence for.

Going for the right level
There are five levels within the NVQ system:

- **Level 1.** Detailing work activities which are mainly routine or provide a broad foundation.

- **Level 2.** Detailing a range of work activities, some complex and non-routine. Candidates must show the ability to work both alone and in collaboration with others.

- **Level 3.** Detailing work activities which are complex and non-routine, possibly involving supervisory competence.

- **Level 4.** Detailing work activities which are complex, technical or professional, including supervision or management and allocation of resources.

- **Level 5.** Detailing the application of complex techniques in an unpredictable range of work situations, together with responsibility for other people's work and the allocation of substantial resources.

BENEFITING FROM APL

Accreditation of prior learning (APL) is a way of being given credit for qualifications and experience you have gained prior to taking an NVQ, so that you don't have to do an entire NVQ.

APL is based on past activities such as full or part-time employment, voluntary work, education and training and leisure activities. APL looks at the *skills*, not the qualifications, you have gained in the past. If current skills match up to an NVQ you want to do now, and valid evidence can be provided, that alone may be enough to credit you for part or all of that unit.

Questions to be answered when considering APL
1. Is the evidence to the required standard of the qualification?

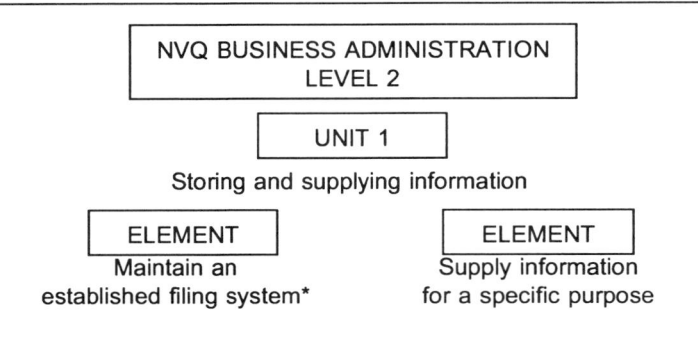

```
┌─────────────────────────────────────────────────────────┐
│              ┌──────────────────────────┐               │
│              │ NVQ BUSINESS ADMINISTRATION │            │
│              │         LEVEL 2          │               │
│              └──────────────────────────┘               │
│                    ┌──────────┐                         │
│                    │  UNIT 1  │                         │
│                    └──────────┘                         │
│             Storing and supplying information           │
│                                                         │
│        ┌───────────┐              ┌───────────┐         │
│        │  ELEMENT  │              │  ELEMENT  │         │
│        └───────────┘              └───────────┘         │
│         Maintain an               Supply information    │
│     established filing system*    for a specific purpose│
│                                                         │
│  * Associated performance criteria                      │
│                                                         │
│  • All file and document movements are controlled and   │
│    recorded accurately.                                 │
│  • All documents are maintained in good condition in    │
│    correct locations.                                   │
│  • Overdue files/documents are identified and system    │
│    for return implemented.                              │
│  • New files are initiated in accordance with           │
│    established system and legibly marked for            │
│    identification.                                      │
│  • All out-of-date documents are identified, extracted  │
│    and dealt with as directed.                          │
│  • Security and confidentiality of information are      │
│    always maintained.                                   │
│  • Safety procedures are followed at all times.         │
└─────────────────────────────────────────────────────────┘
```

Fig. 14. Breakdown of an NVQ element.

```
┌─────────────────────────────────────────────────────────┐
│            **Ways in which you could be assessed**      │
│                                                         │
│  • performing an activity                               │
│  • role play or simulation                              │
│  • a product                                            │
│  • group discussion                                     │
│  • group presentation                                   │
│  • individual presentation                              │
│  • questions                                            │
│  • written multiple choice questions                    │
│  • short written answers                                │
│  • written essays                                       │
│  • projects                                             │
│  • assignments                                          │
│  • diaries                                              │
│  • logs                                                 │
│  • journals                                             │
│  • APL                                                  │
└─────────────────────────────────────────────────────────┘
```

Fig. 15. Methods of assessing a candidate.

Gaining a Qualification and Working Full-Time

2. Can you prove the evidence is yours?

3. Does the evidence apply directly to the NVQ criteria?

4. Is there enough evidence to gain a full credit?

5. Is the evidence recent, *eg* in the last three years?

Evidence you could provide for APL
- letters of reference from a previous employer
- statements from a tutor
- certificates already gained
- examples of past work (signed by someone to acknowledge that it is your own work)
- product examples
- photographic evidence.

ASSESSING COMPETENCE IN THE WORKPLACE

The main thrust of gaining an NVQ is via workplace assessment. A candidate is only assessed when they feel they are ready and in consultation with their assessor.

> The assessment process should be regarded as the process of collecting evidence and making judgements on whether performance criteria has been met. For the award of an NVQ, the candidate must have demonstrated that he/she can meet the performance criteria for each element of competence specified.
> *National Vocational Qualifications: Criteria and Procedures NCVQ 1989*

FINDING EVIDENCE

Successful completion of an NVQ is reliant on you, the candidate, providing evidence. Evidence from various sources is judged against the competence standards laid down.

```
SOURCES OF EVIDENCE ←——→ COMPETENCE STANDARDS
       │
       ▼
Assessment of prior achievement
documents, testimonials
       │
       ▼
Knowledge assessments
multiple choice, essays
       │
       ▼
Performance assessment
workplace assessment, practical tests
```

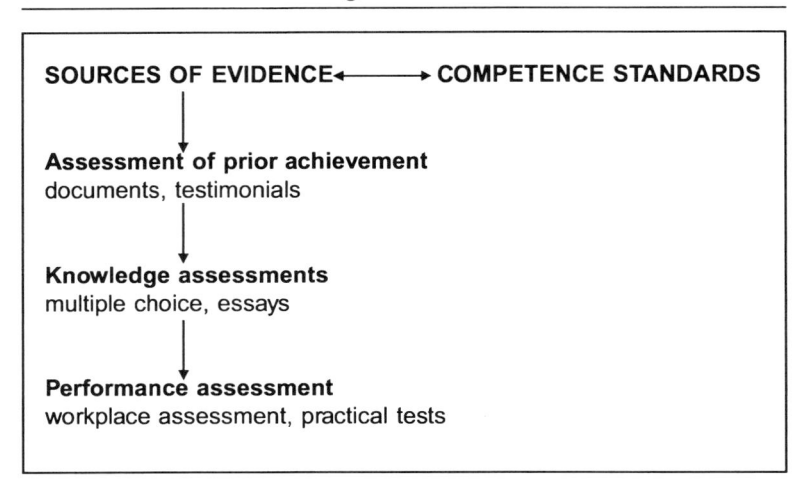

Fig. 16. Finding evidence of competence for NVQs.

BUILDING YOUR PORTFOLIO

A **portfolio** is a way of collecting evidence and proving that you have experience, skills and knowledge for your occupational area. You will need to include compulsory items but you can then choose what you would like included as supporting evidence.

WHO ASSESSES YOU?

The person who will help you through your NVQ is called an **assessor**. They should be qualified to assess people in the workplace and will have taken relevant NVQ units to prove they can assess. Your assessor will be the one who will guide you through putting your portfolio together and who will be 'marking you off' as you successfully provide evidence of your competence.

Where to go next

If you are interested in taking an NVQ, useful contacts might include:

- your local college
- industrial training centres
- commercial training centres
- your local library
- the awarding and examining bodies listed at the end of this book

Gaining a Qualification and Working Full-Time

- your local Training and Enterprise Council (TEC)
- the NCVQ.

CASE STUDIES

Alan goes in-house
The company which Alan works for has its own in-house training scheme which takes some of its structure from the NVQ system, such as providing evidence, workplace assessment, being seen to be doing job-specific tasks. Companies are becoming more geared towards training in the workplace because it is cheaper and doesn't take employees away from their job.

Diane combines learning with work
Diane is intending to work from home. She can build up her qualifications and skills while earning money.

Tony moves on up
Tony is working towards a City and Guilds qualification in the evening. He already has NVQ Level 2 in Telecommunications completed through his company.

Mel is on her own
Mel is training very much in her own time.

DISCUSSION POINTS

1. What NVQs are available for your trade or profession?

2. How would you provide evidence that you could do your job to a complete stranger?

3. How important is the underpinning knowledge upon which the hands-on skills are built?

REASONS FOR TAKING NVQs

1. The standards are set by employers and therefore relate directly to the needs of employment.//
2. Staff become more efficient, thereby making the company more competitive in the global marketplace.
3. The skills level of the workforce is raised, creating more productivity.
4. Staff are more motivated when they see their training relating directly to the workplace.
5. Qualifications can be achieved over a period of time.
6. Learning and assessment is on-going and can happen in the workplace.
7. There are no limitations in terms of where and how to learn.
8. There are clearly defined standards relevant to specific occupations.
9. Candidates have the opportunity to obtain qualifications without specified periods of training.
10. There is no age limit for taking NVQs.
11. There are clear routes for career progression.
12. NVQs say what a candidate can do in a real work situation, not how good they are in exams.
13. There are no pre-entry qualification requirements.
14. NVQs allow the candidate to become more involved in their own training and development.
15. Candidates receive training only on those aspects of the qualifications in which they are not yet competent, so avoiding unnecessary learning.
16. NVQs allows credit for skills and knowledge already gained prior to taking the NVQ.

Fig. 17. Benefits of NVQs.

9
Knowing Who Provides the Training

UNDERSTANDING THE TECs

The Training and Enterprise Councils of England and Wales, and the Enterprise Companies of Scotland, are vital links in the present national training framework and cover all the industries in their area.

The role of the TECs
- To obtain better value for money from public investment in training and enterprise activities by tailoring them to meet the needs of local people and business.

- To secure the commitment of employers to improving the education and training of their own employees.

- To expand opportunities for local people to start their own business and to progress through training.

- To give local employers a key role in running the government's training and enterprise programmes.

TECs work with all companies in all industrial sectors. They also have responsibilities for the unemployed and disadvantaged in the labour market. TECs are responsible for delivering youth and adult training programmes to meet the labour market needs in their locality. They do this by contracting with national and local training providers who can supply the appropriate training course.

LOOKING AT INDUSTRY TRAINING ORGANISATIONS

There are over 120 employer-led **Industry Training Organisations** throughout Great Britain, covering sectors employing around eighty-five per cent of the workforce. These bodies have three roles:

1. Encouraging employers in their industries to increase their training.

2. The monitoring of future skill requirements and training needs in the sector.

3. The development and promotion of occupational standards.

The Industry Training Organisations (ITO) as a whole are represented by the National Council of Industry Training Organisations (NCITO), who in turn have regular contact with government ministers and officials.

Industry related training
Coming down from the Industry Training Organisations are the specialist training companies.

OVERVIEWING BUSINESS SCHOOLS

Until the 1960s the UK was very short of business school education, partially accounting for why less than twenty-five per cent of today's managers have professional and postgraduate management qualifications. Most UK business schools offer:

- MBAs or equivalent degrees

- full- or part-time study

- specialist courses relating to specific industry sectors

- distance learning opportunities

- consortia programmes based on groups of employing organisations

- modular programmes

- executive programmes for the mature student.

The Management Initiative Charter (MIC)
The MIC is designed to improve the performance of UK organisations by improving the quality of UK managers. This

lead body has developed national standards for middle, first-line, supervisory and senior management.

LOOKING INTO FURTHER EDUCATION COLLEGES

Colleges come in two forms, either public or private.

Public FE colleges

Colleges may offer a variety of the following:

- Courses in English as a Foreign Language.

- Adult education (leisure) courses.

- Student services including counselling, careers advice, accommodation service, overseas academic and welfare support advice.

- Library and learning resources.

- Student union.

- Crèche facilities.

- Full- and part-time courses in art, design and media, business and management, catering and hospitality, construction and the built environment, engineering, hair, beauty and community care, humanities and science.

- Flexible (open/distance) learning.

- Staff development programmes catering for business and industry.

- Part-time courses for students with learning difficulties and/or disabilities.

The qualifications offered are always mainstream and geared towards the workplace. Students who are unemployed, in receipt of a means-tested state benefit, or unwaged dependants of the former may have reduced fees. Even if you do have to pay, the fees are usually quite low.

Private colleges
The fees for private schools and colleges are usually a fair bit higher than those of public colleges. If you are considering this option, you need to make sure of the validity of the qualification on offer.

LOOKING INTO UNIVERSITIES

Universities offer a choice of full and part-time degree courses in a wide range of subjects plus:

- help with accommodation
- entertainment
- childcare facilities
- student union
- sport
- counselling
- health services
- career development
- library and resources
- bookshops
- resources for teaching and learning
- computing services.

FINDING OTHER USEFUL ORGANISATIONS

Choosing private management and training consultants
The private training route may be an option to consider. There are many commercial training organisations which would help you get a vocational qualification or learn new job skills.

Costs vary enormously and not all will offer qualifications. Training is usually offered directly to a company, or they may be offered as **open courses**. That means that anyone can come on them.

Taking basic education
Basic education exists everywhere, and every local authority and further education college provides basic education as part of its adult or further education work. There are also some voluntary schemes offering help. It is designed to help people who can't read or write very well, or who have trouble with maths.

It is usually done in a class, a small group or on an individual basis, and can take place in colleges, adult education centres, at work, at home or at a drop-in centre.

Going to a residential college
There are around eight long-term adult residential colleges which provide a route to higher education. They:

- offer educational options as opposed to training, though it may be vocationally geared
- don't require formal entry requirements
- offer courses mainly in humanities and social sciences, and possibly industrial relations and trade union studies.

Looking to the Chamber of Commerce
This organisation runs many short courses during the year, throughout the UK. Local chambers offer courses according to local business need.

Using local enterprise agencies
There are over 400 independent, privately-run local enterprise agencies throughout the UK. They offer advice and support to people wanting to create or develop small businesses. They provide free advice and have access to information on loans. They also provide training.

CASE STUDIES

Alan stays with the company
For as long as Alan stays with the company he is with, he will have free in-house training.

Diane goes private
Diane is taking advantage of private training and is paying for it herself.

Tony returns to college
Tony is mainly taking the further education option which is funded jointly by himself and his company. He is also taking the private training option, as he has bought a software learning pack to help him learn programming at home.

Mel gets it free
Mel is learning through a TEC funded route; her local enterprise

agency provides free one-day seminars on business skills. Her distance learning course is being done through a business school.

DISCUSSION POINTS

1. What should be included in the national curriculum with reference to the world of work?

2. Research the training initiatives that your local TEC is offering. Could any of them be relevant to where you want to get to?

3. If you are working, what links does your company have with local training providers?

10
Making it Happen

Learning happens in order to fulfil a purpose. Sometimes we are taught, other times we learn through trial and error or experience. Three main factors affect *why* and *how* we learn:

- our past learning experiences
- our self-esteem
- our current motivations.

SETTING YOUR PERSONAL LEARNING ACTION PLAN

This section has been influenced by the national **Campaign for Learning**. The campaign is coordinated by the RSA and operates with the TEC National Council, the National Institute of Adult Continuing Education, the Open University and the Scottish Community Education Council, plus other groups and sponsoring companies.

The Campaign for Learning aims to create a learning society in the UK, by encouraging every individual to take an interest in learning and their own personal development.

Reviewing past learning

Look back to four learning experiences in your past (formal or informal) that still have some kind of meaning for you today and ask yourself why they were, and remain, important to you. (See Figure 18.)

Recognising what motivates you

Look over your examples in the exercise in Figure 18. Are you influenced in learning by personal satisfaction and fulfilment, or as a means to an end, or as a stepping stone to something else?

According to your examples, what conditions do you need in order to keep motivated?

WHAT HAVE I LEARNT?			
WHAT	**WHEN**	**WHAT HELPED**	**WHAT HINDERED**
Getting my Certificate in Education	When I was 33	I had done a foundation course in teaching already	The group I went into had already been through the foundation course together, so I felt an outsider
Fill in your own learning experiences			

Fig. 18. Assessing what you have already learnt.

Making it Happen

Getting feedback
In your examples, how important was the encouragement and interest from others? What kind of impact did other people have on your attitude towards learning?

Looking at what you know
Before you can get to somewhere new, you need to know where you are coming from. The exercise in Figure 19 will help you focus on what you already know.

ASSESSING WHERE YOU ARE NOW

Sowing the seeds of your future
What are your hopes with regard to work at this moment? Take this time to look forward and think about where you would like to be, how you would like to live, what you would like to do and the sort of person you want to become.

Questions to ask yourself
- What would I be doing in my work?
- What would my responsibilities be?
- What kind of authority would I have?
- What would my typical working day be like?
- What kind of people would I work with?
- In what kind of surroundings would I work?
- How would my career progress?
- What would my income be?

Choosing your learning future
How might learning fit into your life in the foreseeable future? There are four aspects you might consider:

1. Acquiring new skills, *eg* accounting.
2. Gaining new knowledge, *eg* studying psychology.
3. Learning new attitudes and values, *eg* flexibility.
4. Learning from experience, *eg* foreign travel.

Ask yourself why you want to learn
- To better your performance at work
- To understand something
- To do something
- To succeed in learning something new
- To add a further level of learning to an earlier achievement.

MY LEARNING ACCOUNT		
DIFFERENT EXPERIENCES/ SITUATIONS	EXAMPLES OF WHAT I HAVE LEARNT	EXAMPLES OF HOW IT HAS BEEN RECOGNISED
Work	communication	goods jobs
Being taught	NVQ assessing	C and G certificate
Studying on my own	astrology	teaching at college
Day-to-day living	problem-solving	people ask my help
Home life	taught myself about indoor plants	positive comments on my plant-keeping
Education	religious education	personal growth as an adult

Fig. 19. Assessing your learning, formal and informal.

Making it Happen

FINDING HELP

There are plenty of resources to help you make an informed decision about where to go, and how to find out about courses and funding. Any of the following might prove useful:

your employer
TECs
Jobcentre
public libraries
TAPS (Training and Access Points)

Citizens Advice Bureaux
further education college
career services
university

MOVING FORWARD

Now you are ready to bring together your action plan. Remember to bear in mind your preferred style of learning. Set out:

1. What you intend to learn.
2. How you propose to learn it.
3. When you plan to complete each part of it.

SPECIFIC LEARNING GOAL	HOW I WILL ACHIEVE IT	PROPOSED COMPLETION
To research a qualification in management	Talk to my employer	Within next six months
	Research training providers	Within next six months
	Check out local college	Within next six months
	Research distance learning	Within next six months
To obtain qualification in management	Make a decision based on above and enrol on course	Within next six months
	Completion of course	Within twelve months from enrolment

Fig. 20. Plan of action.

Keep going
When circumstances change you can revise your plan. Keep it updated and under review when key stages occur in your life such as redundancy, applying for promotion, looking for a new job or beginning new training.

LEARNING FOR LIFE

My own path of learning has been diverse. I had a normal educational background culminating in four O-Levels. My learning experiences at school weren't brilliant. I enjoyed religious education, English and art more than anything else (these were my O-Levels). From when I left school until I was 30 my learning occurred through hands-on job experience or, as with astrology, I taught myself.

When I was 30 I went back to part-time study to formalise my teaching experience and get a piece of paper from C and G. Then, because I wasn't sure whether I wanted to be a counsellor or teacher, I took a part-time counselling certificate. I decided I wanted to be a teacher, so I took the Certificate of Education to round up my teaching qualifications. Under the auspices of a commercial training company where I had a contract, I took the NVQ D units in assessing. Recently I almost took an NVQ in management but decided it would be too much work along with everything else at the time.

I came into learning late. As a teacher, I think I was frightened to become a student! Learning as an adult is very different from learning as a young person. *It is much more rewarding.* I learn because I want to. I never want to stop learning. I can't stop learning; nor can you. It just depends on whether the learning is formal or informal. If you stopped learning, you'd be numb. The fact that you are reading this book indicates you want to learn. Now you've completed the book, you have learnt more about the facts, attitudes and values of vocational learning. Are you curious to know more?

Then get out there and start finding out for yourself. Good luck.

CASE STUDIES

Alan is where the action is
When I was researching this book I phoned Alan to check about his in-house training. He sounded motivated and enthusiastic. He's making it happen right now. He's doing what he wants to be doing and that is the motivation for wanting to learn more.

Diane is in business

Diane has taken an examination in book-keeping and passed with flying colours. She is still learning French and she has started an OU course in business studies. At this point she has three clients for whom she does the books. She has ambitions to train as a business counsellor some time in the future. She has a reason for valuing herself now.

Tony has developed new interests

Tony is coming to the end of his further education course in computer-aided engineering. He wants to consolidate his new learning through his workplace. He is writing software programs for the entertainment industry in his spare time and is beginning to build up new contacts. He feels better about his paid work now, and isn't so stressed because he is building up outside interests with a view to moving on.

Mel has broken the glass ceiling

Mel is working freelance for two management consultancies. She is using the distance learning in a real work environment. Now she is considering taking NVQ Management Level 4 with one of the companies she works for.

DISCUSSION POINTS

1. Where do you see yourself in ten years from now?

2. What new things have you learnt in the last week?

3. What have you learnt from this book?

Glossary

Accreditation. The official recognition of a person, having successfully gained a qualification, or an organisation, having reached a level of delivering training courses. A guarantee of quality.

Action plan. Occurs as part of the process of change. When we have thought through a course of action, we then need to plan the specific steps needed to make that action happen.

Adult bursaries. A form of funding usually available from your local careers office. If you are claiming benefit and the course which you want funding comes within the stated criteria, you may get part or all of your course paid for.

Assessment. Term linked to NVQs. In workplace assessment a candidate taking an NVQ is observed doing the task involved in a job, thereby creating evidence for assessment leading to an NVQ.

Assignment. A task allocated to a student reflecting their learning.

Awarding body. Official bodies which award certificates, diplomas and NVQs such as City and Guilds or RSA.

Benefit system. The formal system, put in place by the government which allocates financial resources for special needs, *eg* if a person is unemployed, has a family.

Block/day release. People in full-time employment and studying for a qualification are usually required to be released from work one day or more per week to attend college.

Campus. A university layout covering residential halls, lecture rooms, shops, libraries, entertainment places, *etc*.

Career development. A personal path which involves the carefully laid out development of skills and knowledge.

Career development loans. Loans to help pay for training.

Careers office. Usually found in every major town. They offer careers guidance specifically for young people, but with an increasing emphasis on adults. They usually have an occupational library and give advice on retraining.

Glossary

Claimant advisers. Personnel who work in Jobcentres. They are available to help with any benefit queries and vacancy advice.

Continuous learning programme. A programme of learning which the individual is setting for themselves in order to improve their skills and knowledge.

Core competencies. A proven skill or knowledge base which can be built upon or transferred between occupations, *eg* customer care.

Core skills. With reference to GNVQs, refers to the levels of basic skills which are required to complete the level.

Coursework assignments. Project work which is set during a course and reflects your knowledge, plus developing the actual skills involved in putting together an assignment.

Customer care. Customer relations, complaint handling.

CV. *Curriculum vitae.* Your work history.

Dependants. Children, or aged parents or relatives who are dependent on you for care. This caring role may influence the time available for work or study.

Developmental skills. Skills used to move on a project.

Essay. A literary composition on any subject.

Examining and awarding bodies. Organisations such as City and Guilds which set national standards and award qualifications.

Facilitator. Someone who informally guides the learning process so that the student discovers for themselves (a teacher or tutor tells the student).

Foundation course. Usually refers to a university-type course and describes a course taken prior to the actual qualification.

Government schemes. The Jobcentre offers a wide variety of schemes designed specifically to help people return to work. Free to people on benefit.

In-house. Keeping it in the company.

Interpersonal skills. How we relate and communicate with each other.

IT. Information technology.

Job-search skills. The skills necessary to market our strengths and experience in a fast-moving world of work: *eg* CV writing, interview techniques.

Job-specific skills. Skills directly related to specific tasks, *eg* word processing.

Jobcentre. Usually in every major town, Jobcentres are part of the Civil Service and offer a wide range of services such as advertised vacancies, retraining opportunities, job-search workshops, information on funding.

Knowledge-based. Knowledge needed to do a job-specific skill, *eg* to do word processing we need to know about disk management.
Linguistic and cultural skills. Skills necessary to communicate with other countries.
Literacy. Reading and writing skills.
Mandatory. With reference to GNVQs, units which must be taken.
Motivation. Inner drive, our reason for doing something, why we think, feel and behave as we do.
Multi-skilled. To be skilled in several (possible related) areas of work, *eg* word processing, administrative and desk-top publishing skills.
Peers. People of the same generation.
Performance criteria. Used in the NVQ structure to refer to the standards a candidate needs to meet in the tasks they perform.
Prospectus. Yearly or half-yearly documents detailing courses from adult education, further education and universities.
Re-skill. The re-training process; an updating of skills to meet current requirements.
Seminars. A learning situation which is not normally participatory.
Single-skilled. Having a particular skill which is not easily transferable.
Simulation. With reference to being assessed for an NVQ, this term is applied when evidence cannot be obtained from the workplace; a role-play situation has to be set up.
Skills assessment. We need to be aware of our skills so that we can sell ourselves through our CV and during an interview. Also necessary when considering a change of career. Skills usually means work-related plus those skills we have built up outside of work that may be relevant, *eg* treasurer, writing.
Skills. When we use our skills, we are demonstrating through doing something.
Study skills. When teaching ourselves or being taught, part of the process is using effective study skills which develop the ability for note-taking, writing essays and projects.
Summer school. The Open University in particular has summer schools as part of its curriculum. Usually a residential week of learning held in the middle of the year.
Synopsis. An overview of a subject.
Synthesis. A building up of separate elements of a project into a connected whole.
TAPS. Training and Access Points. Computer-aided guidance to find vocational training. Available in your local library or careers

centre.
Technology. Any equipment using electricity or batteries, *eg* a production line, computers, printing presses or calculators.
TECs. Training and Enterprise Council (local address in the phone book). Provides skill-based training for business.
Tertiary. The next educational institution after secondary school.
Thesis. A document prepared by a student for their degree.
Training. This type of learning is usually skills-based and work-related.
Tutorials. Individual or group sessions at educational institutions to discuss your thoughts and feelings about the course and your performance.
Visual aids. Aids to assist when giving a presentation or training. They might include flip-charts, overhead projectors, hand-outs, slide projectors, whiteboards or blackboards.
Vocational skills. Skills related to an occupational area.
Work experience. Usually related to taking a vocational qualification whereby the candidate or trainee has experience of working in a commercial or industrial environment during part of their study time.
Work history. Who we have worked for, what we did and when. It is required on your CV and on application forms.
Workplace assessment. When you take an NVQ the evidence is gathered from your workplace, so that you can see the direct relevance to your job. Workplace assessment is direct observation of you doing particular job-specific tasks.
Work-related. Courses being offered are increasingly being related to a working environment.
Workshops. A practical, hands-on learning experience.

Further Reading

DIRECTORIES

Directory of Educational Guidance Services for Adults, FEU, Citadel Place, Tinworth Street, London SE11 5EH.
Directory of Further Education, Biblios PDS Ltd, Start Road, Partridge Green, West Sussex RH13 8LD.
Directory of Grant Making Trusts, (Charities Aid Foundation). List of funds available for research, education and training.
Education Grants Directory, Michael Eastwood and David Casson (Directory of Social Change).
Kelly's Business Directory, Information on over 82,000 industrial, commercial and professional organisations in the UK.
The Open Learning Directory 1996, (Pergamon Open Learning). Lists hundreds of open learning packages for most vocational areas.

FUNDING

A Guide to Grants for Individuals in Need, The Directory of Social Change, Radius Works, Back Lane, London NW3 1HL. Lists grant-making charities for particular illnesses or disabilities.
Department of Education, Publications Centre, PO Box 2193, London E15 2EU. Tel: (0181) 533 2000. Information on grants.
MRC, Project Grants, 20 Park Crescent, London W1N 4AL. Research and training opportunities and project grants.
Sponsorships 1995, COIC, Department CW, ISCO5, The Paddock, Frizinghall, Bradford BD9 4HD.
Student Grants and Loans, Department for Education, Sanctuary Buildings, Great Smith Street, London SW1P 3BT.
Student Loan Company Ltd, 100 Bothwell Street, Glasgow G2 7GD. Tel: (01345) 300 900. Booklet on loans to students.
Students' Money Matters, (Trotman).

Tax Relief for Vocational Training, Personnel Taxpayers Leaflet IR 119 (Inland Revenue).
The Grant Register, (Macmillan Press).

GENERAL CAREERS INFORMATION

Changing your Job after 35, Godfrey Golzen (Kogan Page, 1994).
Handbook of Free Careers Information in the UK, (Trotman, 1993).
Job Ideas, (COIC).
Job Search Guide, CEPEC Ltd, Princes House, 36 Jermyn Street, London SW1Y 6DN. For executives and professionals.
Jobs for the Over 50s, Linda Greenbury (Piatkus, 1994).
Just the Job, John Best (Nicholas Brealey, 1994).
Occupations 96, Careers and Occupation Information, PO Box 348, Bristol BS99 7FE. Wide range of publications and booklets on career options.
Offbeat Careers, Vivien Donald (Kogan Page, 1995).

SPECIAL NEEDS STUDENTS

Adult Literacy and Basic Skills Unit, Kingsbourne House, 229-231 Holborn, London WC1V 7DA. Tel: (0171) 405 4017.
Adults with Learning Difficulties: curriculum choice and empowerment, Jeannie Sutcliffe (Open University Press).

STUDENT SERVICES

Students Guide to Credit Accumulation and Transfer, ECCTIS 2000 Ltd, Fulton House, Hessop Avenue, Cheltenham, Gloucestershire GL50 3SH.

STUDY SKILLS

How to Study and Learn, Peter Marshall (How To Books, 1995).
How to Study Effectively, Richard Freeman and John Meed (National Extension College, 1993).
The Good Study Guide, Andrew Nortledge (Open University).

TV AND RADIO

On Course, BBC Education Information, G422, BBC White City, 201 Wood Lane, London W12 7TS. A guide to BBC continuing education.

QUALIFICATIONS

A Guide to Higher Education Systems and Qualifications in the European Community, (Kogan Page).
British Qualifications (Kogan Page, 1994). A guide to educational, technical, professional and academic qualifications in Britain.
British Vocation Qualifications (Kogan Page, 1995). A directory of vocational qualifications available from all awarding bodies in Britain.
Degree Course Guides, (CRAC, Hobsons Press, bi-annually).
Directory of Further Education, the comprehensive guide to courses in UK polytechnics and colleges, James Tomlinson and David Weigall (CRAC, Hobsons Press, annually).
Getting into University and College, (Trotman).
Getting into Vocational Qualifications, (Trotman).
How to Choose your Degree Course, Brian Heap (Trotman).
Returning to Work: a directory of educational training for women, Womens Returners Network (Kogan Page).
Second Chances: guide to adult education and training opportunities (COIC, 1993).
Unemployment Unit, 322 St John Street, London EC1V 4NT. Unemployment and training rights handbook.

Useful Addresses

AWARDING BODIES

Business and Technology Education Council (BTEC), Central House, Upper Woburn Place, London WC1H 0HH. Tel: (0171) 413 8400. Information on BTEC courses.

City and Guilds of London Institute, Marketing and PR Department, 326 City Road, London EC1V 2PT. Tel: (0171) 278 2468. Information on C and G courses including NVQs.

Examinations of the Pitmans Examinations Institute, Catteshall Manor, Godalming, Surrey GU7 1UU. Tel: (01483) 415311.

London Chamber of Commerce and Industry Examinations Board, Marlowe House, Station Road, Sidcup, Kent DA15 7BJ. Tel: (0181) 302 0261. Information on administration, management and business qualifications.

National Council for Vocational Qualifications, 222 Euston Road, London NW1 2BZ. Tel: (0171) 387 9898. Information on NVQs.

RSA Examinations Board, Westwood Way, Coventry CV4 8HS. Tel: (01203) 470033.

Scottish Vocational Education Council (SCOTVEC), Hanover House, 24 Douglas Street, Glasgow G2 7NQ. Tel: (0141) 248 7900. Information on qualifications.

CAREERS INFORMATION

Careers and Occupation Information Centre, PO Box 348, Bristol BS99 7FE. Tel: (0117) 9777199. Publications and booklets.

Careers Office. Your local *Yellow Pages*.

Jobcentres. Your local *Yellow Pages*.

Skill: National Bureau for Students with Disabilities, 336 Brixton Road, London SW9 7AA. Tel: (0171) 274 0565. Develops opportunities in further and higher education and employment for those with disabilities or learning difficulties.

COURSE AND TRAINING INFORMATION

British Accreditation Council for Independent Further and Higher Education, Middlesex University, White Hart Lane, London N17 8HR. Tel: (0181) 362 6218.

ECCTIS 2000, Fulton House, Jessop Avenue, Cheltenham, Gloucester GL50 3SH. Tel: (01242) 518724. Computer databases found in colleges, careers offices, adult guidance services and libraries giving information on around 100,000 courses in the UK.

National Training Federation, PO Box 1, Atherstone, Warwickshire CV9 1BE. Tel: (01827) 716735. Provides information on specialist industrial training organisations which provide training for a particular job or industry.

Training Access Points (TAPS), St Mary's House, c/o Moorfoot, Sheffield S1 4PQ.

Workers' Educational Association (WEA), Temple House, 17 Victoria Park Square, Bethnal Green, London E2 9PB. Tel: (0181) 983 1515.

DISABLED STUDENTS (RESIDENTIAL AND NON-RESIDENTIAL)

Doncaster College for the Deaf, Leger Way, Doncaster, South Yorkshire DN2 6AY. Tel: (01302) 22822. BTEC, NVQ, GNVQ, City and Guilds, RSA, GCSE and A-Levels in art and design, brickwork, business studies, caring, carpentry and joinery, catering, computing, electronics, engineering, floristry, hairdressing, land skills, painting and decorating and vehicle bodywork repair.

Education, Training and Employment Department, MENCAP, 123 Golden Lane, London EC1Y 0RT. Tel: (0171) 454 0454.

Finchale Training College, Durham DH1 5RX. Tel: (0191) 386 2634. Courses in business administration, office machine servicing, watch and clock repair, horticulture, financial accounting, computer application, electronic servicing, bench joinery and assistant quantity surveying.

Lincolnshire College of Agriculture and Horticulture, Riseholme Hall, Riseholme, Lincoln LN2 2LG. Tel: (01522) 522252.

Portland Training College, Nottingham Road, Mansfield, Nottingham NG18 4TJ. Tel: (01623) 792141. Courses similar to Finchale plus life and social skills, independent living, literacy and numeracy.

Queen Alexandra College, Court Oak Road, Harbourne, Birmingham B17 9TG. Tel: (0121) 428 5050. Courses on production assembly, craft and design, glass engraving, engineering, cycle mechanics, telephony, reception, retail and information processing.

Queen Elizabeth's Training College, Leatherhead Court, Leatherhead, Surrey KT22 0BN. Tel: (01372) 842204. Courses similar to Finchale plus audio-visual technician, travel and tourism, industrial sewing machining, spray painting, engineering design and draughtmanship.

RNIB Redhill College, Philanthropic Road, Redhill, Surrey RH1 4DZ. Tel: (01737) 768935. Courses in office and business skills, cycle maintenance and repairs, craft design and technology, horticulture and floristry, community care, musician training, information technology, manufacturing practice and stenography.

Royal National College for the Blind, College Road, Hereford HR1 1EB. Tel: (01432) 265725. Courses in business and secretarial skills, computer applications and programming, art and design, music and music technology, remedial therapy, piano tuning and repairs.

St Loyes College Foundation, Fairfield House, Topsham Road, Exeter, Devon EX2 6EP. Tel: (01392) 55428. Courses similar to Finchale plus food preparation, butchery and cookery.

FUNDING

Awards Officer, Adult Education Bursaries, Ruskin College, Oxford OX1 2HE. Tel: (01865) 56360.

Career Development Loans, Freepost, PO Box 99, Sudbury, Suffolk CO10 6BR. Freephone 0800 585505.

Department of Health, Student Grants Unit, Morcross, Blackpool FY5 3TA. Tel: (01253) 856123. Grants for occupational therapy, physiotherapy, radiography, dentistry.

Department for Education, Sanctuary Buildings, Great Smith Street, London SW1P 3BT. Tel: (0171) 925 5000.

Educational Grants Advisory Service, Family Welfare Association, 501/505 Kingsland Road, London E8.

Local Education Authorities (LEA). Your local *Yellow Pages*. Mandatory and discretionary grants.

Project 2000. Your local health authority. Bursaries for nursing.

The Student Loans Company, 100 Bothwell Street, Glasgow G2 7JD. Tel: (01345) 300900.

INDUSTRY LEAD BODIES

Advice, Guidance, Counselling and Psychotherapy Lead Body, 40a High Street, Welwyn, Hertfordshire AL6 9EQ. Tel: (01438) 840511.

Amenity Horticulture Lead Body, Local Government Management Board, Arndale House, Arndale Centre, Luton LU1 2TS. Tel: (01582) 451166.

Arts and Entertainment Training Council, 3 St Peters Building, York Street, Leeds LS9 8AJ. Tel: (0113) 244 8845.

Association of Accounting Technicians, 154 Clerkenwell Road, London EC1R 5AD. Tel: (0171) 837 8600.

Association of British Travel Agents National Training Board, The Cornerstone, The Broadway, Woking, Surrey GU21 5AR. Tel: (01483) 727321.

Association of the British Pharmaceutical Industry, 12 Whitehall, London SW1A 2DY. Tel: (0171) 930 3477.

Aviation Training Association, 125 London Road, High Wycombe, Buckinghamshire HP11 1BT. Tel: (01494) 445262.

Banking Industry Training Council, 10 Lombard Street, London EC3V 9AT. Tel: (0171) 398 4246.

Biscuit, Cake, Chocolate and Confectionery Alliance, 37-41 Bedford Row, London WC1R 4JH. Tel: (0171) 404 9111.

Board of Education and Training for the Water Industry, 1 Queen Anne's Gate, London SW1H 9BT. Tel: (0171) 957 4524.

Books Training Centre, 45 East Hill, Wandsworth, London SW18 2QZ. Tel: (0181) 874 2718. Editorial lead body.

British Agricultural and Garden Machinery Association, Church Street, Rickmansworth, Hertfordshire WD3 1RQ. Tel: (01923) 720241.

British Plumbing Employers' Council, c/o SNIPEF, 2 Walker Street, Edinburgh EH3 7LB. Tel: (0131) 225 2255.

British Footwear Manufacturers' Federation, 5 Portland Place, London W1N 3AA. Tel: (0171) 580 8687.

British Furniture Manufacturers' Training Ltd, 30 Harcourt Street, London W1H 2AA. Tel: (0171) 724 0851.

British Gas plc, 3rd Floor, 100 Rochester Row, London SW1P 1JP. Tel: (0171) 821 1444.

British Nuclear Fuels plc, Risley, Warrington WA3 6AS. Tel:

(01925) 832000.
British Ports Industry Training Ltd, PO Box 555, Bury St Edmunds, Suffolk IP28 6QG. Tel: (01284) 811555.
British Printing Industries Federation Training Organisation, 11 Bedford Row, London WC1R 4DX. Tel: (0171) 242 6904.
Building Services Engineering Development Group Consortium, Gear House, Salt Meadows Road, Gateshead NE8 3AH. Tel: (0191) 490 1155.
Building Societies Association, 3 Savile Row, London W1X 1AF. Tel: (0171) 437 0655.
Bus and Coach Training Ltd, Regency House, 43 High Street, Rickmansworth, Hertfordshire WD3 1ET. Tel: (01923) 896607.
CAPITB Brust, 80 Richardshaw Lane, Pudsey, Leeds LS28 6BN. Tel: (0113) 239 3355. Clothing lead body.
Chemical Industries Association Ltd, Kings Building, Smith Square, London SW1P 3JJ. Tel: (0171) 834 3399.
CISC, The Building Centre, 26 Store Street, London WC1E 7BT. Tel: (0171) 323 5270. Civil engineering lead body.
Construction Industry Training Board, Bircham Newton, Nr Kings Lynn, Norfolk PE31 6RH. Tel: (01553) 776677.
COSQUEC, The Red House, Pillows Green, Staunton, Gloucestershire GL19 3NU. Tel: (01452) 840825. Environmental conservation lead body.
Craft Occupational Standard Board, Robert House, Station Approach, Romsey, Hampshire SO51 8DU. Tel: (01794) 513424.
Customer Service Lead Body, 132 Newport Road, Stafford ST16 1AA. Tel: (01785) 226328.
Dairy Trade Federation, 19 Cornwall Terrace, London NW1 4QP. Tel: (0171) 486 7244.
Industrial Lead Body for Design, 29 Bedford Square, London WC1B 3EG. Tel: (0171) 486 1510.
Distilling Industry Vocational Qualifications Group, 20 Atholl Crescent, Edinburgh EH3 8HF. Tel: (0131) 221 0202.
Distributive OSC, Bedford House, 69-79 Fulham High Street, London SW6 3JW. Tel: (0171) 371 7673. Betting lead body.
Electrical and Electronics Servicing, Savoy Hill House, Savoy Hill, London WC2R 0BS. Tel: (0171) 836 3357.
Electricity Training Association, 30 Millbank, London SW1P 4RD. Tel: (0171) 344 5770.
Electronic Office Systems Maintenance Lead Body, c/o EEB, Savoy Hill House, Savoy Hill, London WC2R 0BS. Tel: (0171) 836 3357.
Engineering Training Authority, Vector House, 41 Clarendon Road,

Watford WD1 1HS. Tel: (01923) 238441.

Fire Industry Lead Body Secretariat, 10 Bluebell Drive, Burghfield Common, Reading RG7 3EF. Tel: (01734) 833342.

Food and Drink Qualifications Council, 6 Catherine Street, London WC2B 5JJ. Tel: (0171) 836 2460.

Forensic Science Sector, Priory House, Gooch Street North, Birmingham B5 6QQ. Tel: (0121) 666 6606.

Forestry and Arboriculture Safety Training Council, Forestry Commission, 231 Corstorphine Road, Edinburgh EH12 7AT. Tel: (0131) 334 8083.

Gamekeeping and Fish Husbandry, Valley Farm, Stock, Andover, Hampshire SP11 0NR. Tel: (01264) 738311.

Glass Training Ltd, BGMC Building, Northumberland Road, Sheffield S10 2UA. Tel: (0114) 266 1494.

Hairdressing Training Board, 3 Chequer Road, Doncaster DN1 2AA. Tel: (01302) 342837.

HBTTB, PO Box 21, Bognor Regis, West Sussex PO21 2PF. Tel: (01243) 860339. Health and beauty lead body.

Heating and Ventilation Contractors' Association, Gear House, Saltmeadows Road, Gateshead, NE8 3AH. Tel: (0191) 490 1155.

Hotel and Catering Training Company, International House, High Street, Ealing, London W5 5DB. Tel: (0181) 579 2400.

Housing Sector Consortium, Arndale House, The Arndale Centre, Luton LU1 2TS. Tel: (01582) 451166.

Information and Library Services Lead Body, 7 Ridgemount Street, London WC1E 7AE. Tel: (0171) 255 2271.

Institute of Chartered Secretaries and Administrators, 16 Park Crescent, London W1N 4AH. Tel: (0171) 753 0727.

Institute of Maintenance and Building Management, Keets House, 30 East Street, Farnham, Surrey GU9 7SW. Tel: (01252) 710994.

Insurance Industry Training Council, Churchill Court, 90 Kippington Road, Sevenoaks, Kent TN13 2LL. Tel: (01732) 741231.

International Trade and Services Lead Body, British Chambers of Commerce, 4 Westwood House, Westwood Business Park, Coventry CV4 8HS. Tel: (01203) 694492.

Jewellery and Allied Industries Lead Body, British Jewellers Association, 10 Vyse Street, Birmingham B18 6LT. Tel: (0121) 236 2651.

Joint National Horse Education and Training Council, Stainton Woodhouse, Lime Kiln Lane, Stainton, Rotherham S66 7QY. Tel: (01709) 813458.

Languages Lead Body, c/o Centre for Information on Language

Useful Addresses

Teaching and Research, 20 Bedfordbury, London WC2N 4LB. Tel: (0171) 379 5134.

Management Charter Initiative, Russell Square House, 10-12 Russell Square, London WC1B 5BZ. Tel: (0171) 872 9000.

Marketing Services Board, 49a High Street, Yeadon, Leeds LS19 7SP. Tel: (0113) 250 8955.

Merchant Navy Training Board, Carthusian Court, 12 Carthusian Street, London EC1M 6EB. Tel: (0171) 417 8400.

Mining Industry Lead Body, c/o Education and Training Branch, Eastwood Coal, Eastwood Hall, Eastwood, Nottingham NG16 3EB. Tel: (01773) 532111.

Motor Industry Training Standards Council, 201 Great Portland Street, London W1N 6AB. Tel: (0171) 436 6373.

Museum Training Institute, Kershaw House, 55 Well Street, Bradford BD1 5PS. Tel: (01274) 391056.

National Retail Training Council, 4th Floor, Bedford House, 66-79 Fulham High Street, London SW6 3JW. Tel: (0171) 371 5021.

National Textile Training Group, Jarodale House, 7 Gregory Boulevard, Nottingham NG7 6LD. Tel: (0115) 953 1866.

Newspaper Society, Bloomsbury House, Bloomsbury Square, 74-77 Great Russell Street, London WC1B 3DA. Tel: (0171) 636 7014.

Occupational Health and Safety Lead Body, Health and Safety Executive, 7th Floor, Rose Court, 2 Southwark Bridge, London SE1 9HF. Tel: (0171) 717 6000.

Offshore Petroleum ITO, Inchbroach House, South Quay, Montrose DD10 9SL. Tel: (01674) 662500.

Pensions Management Institute, PMI House, 4-10 Artillery Lane, London E1 7LS. Tel: (0171) 247 1452.

Personnel Standards Lead Body, 2 Savoy Court, Strand, London WC2R 0SZ. Tel: (0171) 240 7474.

Pest Control Lead Body, British Pest Control Association, 3 St James Court, Friar Gate, Derby DE1 1ZU. Tel: (01332) 294288.

Photography and Photographic Processing ITO, Peel Place, 50 Carver Street, Hockley, Birmingham B1 3AS. Tel: (0121) 212 0299.

Police Services Lead Body, 15 Delacourt Road, London SE3 8XA. Tel: (0181) 350 1027.

Prison Services Lead Body, 15 Delacourt Road, London SE3 8XA. Tel: (0181) 305 1027.

Purchasing and Supply Lead Body, Easton House, Easton on the Hill, Stamford, Lincolnshire PE9 3NZ. Tel: (01780) 56777.

Rail Industry Training Council, 8th Floor, Euston House, 24

Eversholt Street, London NW1 1DZ. Tel: (0171) 320 0436.
Refrigeration Industry Board, 76 Mill Lane, Carshalton, Surrey SM5 2JR. Tel: (0181) 647 7033.
Residential Estate Agency Training and Education Association, The Avenue, Brampford, Speke, Exeter EX5 5DW. Tel: (01392) 841194.
Road Haulage and Distribution Training Council, Shenley Hall, Rectory Lane, Radlett, Hertfordshire WD7 9AN. Tel: (01923) 858461.
Sales Qualifications Board, 29 Floral Street, London WC2E 9DP. Tel: (0171) 497 1234.
Security Industry Lead Body, Security House, Barbourne Road, Worcester WR1 1RS. Tel: (01905) 20004.
Skillset, 124 Horseferry Road, London SW1P 2TX. Tel: (0171) 306 8585. Broadcasting and film lead body.
Sport and Recreation Lead Body, c/o The Sports Council, 16 Upper Woburn Place, London WC1H 0QP. Tel: (0171) 388 1277.
Standard Conference for Engineering Manufacture, c/o The Institution of Electrical Engineers, Savoy Place, London WC2R 0RL. Tel: (0171) 240 1871.
Standard Conference for Engineering Services, c/o The Institution of Marine Engineers, The Memorial Building, 76 Mark Lane, London EC3R 7JN. Tel: (0171) 481 8493.
Training and Development Lead Body, c/o Employment Occupational Standards Council, 2 Savoy Court, The Strand, London WC2R 0EZ. Tel: (0171) 240 6264.
TVSC, 399 South Row, Milton Keynes MK9 2PG. Tel: (01908) 240120. Telecommunications lead body.
Veterinary Lead Body, The Royal College of Veterinary Surgeons, 32 Belgrave Square, London SW1X 8QP. Tel: (0171) 235 4971.
Wood Green Animal Shelters, King's Bush Farm, London Road, Huntingdon, Cambridgeshire PE18 8LJ. Tel: (01480) 831177. Animal care lead body.

OLDER STUDENTS

University of the Third Age, 1 Stockwell Green, London SW9 9JF.

OPEN LEARNING

Council for the Accreditation of Correspondence Colleges (CACC), 27 Marylebone Road, London NW1 5JS. Tel: (0171) 935 5391.
Insight Information, BBC, Broadcasting House, London W1A 1AA. Learning from home via the TV.

Useful Addresses

International Correspondence Schools, 8 Elliot Place, Glasgow G3 8EF. Tel: (0141) 221 2926.

National Extension College, 18 Brooklands Avenue, Cambridge CB2 2HN. Tel: (01223) 316644. Study skills, GCSEs, A-Levels, degrees, professional studies and languages.

Open College, St Paul's, 781 Wilmslow Road, Didsbury, Manchester M20 8RW. Tel: (0161) 434 0007. Work-related courses including work skills, management and supervision, accountancy, health and care, technology, and education and training.

Open College of the Arts, Houndhill, Worsbrough, Barnsley, South Yorkshire S70 6TU. Tel: (01891) 168902. Art and design, creative writing, drawing, garden design, music, painting, photography, sculpture and textiles.

Open University, PO Box 71, Milton Keynes MK7 6AG.

Radio Publicity, BBC, Broadcasting House, London W1A 1AA. Tel: (0171) 580 4468. Learning from home via the radio.

PRISONERS AND EX-OFFENDERS

National Association for the Care and Resettlement of Offenders (NACRO) National Education Advisory Service, 567a Barlow Moor Road, Manchester M21 2AE. Information and advice on colleges, courses and grants.

RESIDENTIAL COLLEGES

Ruskin College, Walaton Street, Oxford OX1 2HE. Tel: (01865) 54331. Diploma courses and major subjects including labour studies, French communication, languages and women's studies.

Plater Colleges, Pullens Lane, Oxford OX3 0DT. Tel: (01865) 74176. Special diploma in social administration or social studies. College diploma in theology and social studies and college certificate in social studies for pastoral ministry.

Northern College, Wentworth Castle, Stainborough, Barnsley, South Yorkshire S75 3ET. Tel: (01226) 285426. College certificate and diploma in trade union and industrial studies, social and community studies and liberal and gateway studies.

STUDENT SERVICES

Association of Commonwealth Universities, John Foster House, 36 Gordon Square, London WC1. Tel: (0171) 387 8572.

Central Bureau for Educational Visits and Exchanges, Seymour Mews House, Seymour Mews, London W1H 9PE. Tel: (0171) 486 5101.
National Bureau for Students with Disabilities, 336 Brixton Road, London SW9 7AA. Tel: (0171) 274 0565.
National Institute of Adult Continuing Education, Charles Street Adult Education Centre, Charles Street, Luton LU2 OEB. Tel: (01582) 22566.
UCAS (Universities and Colleges Admissions Service), PO Box 67, Cheltenham, Gloucestershire GL50 3SF. Tel: (01242) 227788.
United Kingdom Council for Overseas Student Affairs, 9-17 St Albans Place, London N1 ONX. Tel: (0171) 226 3762.

VOCATIONAL

Business services and sales
Association of Accounting Technicians, 154 Clerkenwell Road, London EC1R 5AD. Tel: (0171) 837 8600. Professional training.
Association of Cost and Executive Accountants, Tower House, 141-149 Fonthill Road, London N4 3HF. (0171) 272 3925. Professional qualifications and professional membership.
Association of Legal Secretaries, The Mill, Clymping Street, Clymping, Littlehampton, West Sussex BN17 5RN. Tel: (01243) 820475. Professional qualifications and information.
Association of Certified Book-keepers, PO Box 1170, London N11 1TL. Professional training and professional membership.
Association of Conference Executives, Riverside House, High Street, Huntingdon, Cambridgeshire PE18 6SG. Tel: (01480) 457595. Professional membership and training.
British Institute of Professional Photography, Fox Talbot House, 2 Amwell End, Ware, Hertfordshire SG12 9HN. Tel: (01920) 464011. Professional qualifications and professional membership.
British International Freight Association (incorporating the Institute of Freight Forwarders), Redfern House, Browells Lane, Feltham, Middlesex TW13 7EP. Tel: (0181) 844 2266. Professional qualifications, careers information and professional membership.
Chartered Association of Certified Accountants, 29 Lincoln's Inn Fields, London WC2A 3EE. Tel: (0171) 396 5700. Professional qualifications and professional membership.
Chartered Institute of Bankers, 10 Lombard Street, London EC3V 9AS. Tel: (0171) 623 3531. Professional training and professional membership.
Chartered Institute of Management Accountants, 63 Portland

Place, London W1N 4AB. Tel: (0171) 637 2311. Professional training and careers information.

Chartered Institute of Marketing, Moor Hall, Cookham, Maidenhead, Berkshire SL6 9QH. Tel: (01628) 524922. Professional training and professional membership.

Chartered Institute of Purchasing and Supply, Easton House, Easton on the Hill, Stamford, Lincolnshire PE9 3NZ. Tel: (01780) 56777. Professional qualifications and information.

Chartered Insurance Institute, 2 Aldermanbury, London EC2V 7HY. Tel: (0171) 606 3835. Careers information and professional training.

Communication Advertising and Marketing Education Foundation, Abford House, 15 Wilton Road, London SW1V 1NJ. Tel: (0171) 828 7506. Professional training.

General Council of the Bar (Barristers), Education and Training, 2-3 Cursitor Street, London EC4A 1NE. Tel: (0171) 440 4000.

Institute of Administrative Management, 40 Chatsworth Parade, Petts Wood, Orpington, Kent BR5 1RW. Tel: (01689) 875555. Professional training and professional management.

Institute of Employment Consultants, 6 Guildford Road, Woking, Surrey GU22 7PX. Professional training and professional membership.

Institute of Information Scientists, 44-45 Museum Street, London WC1A 1LY. Tel: (0171) 831 8003. Professional membership and careers information.

Institute of Legal Executives, Kempston Manor, Kempston, Bedford MK42 7AB. Tel: (01234) 841000. Professional qualifications and information.

Institute of Linguists, 24a Highbury Grove, London N5 2DQ. Tel: (0171) 359 7445. Professional qualifications and information.

Institute of Management Services, 1 Cecil Court, London Road, Enfield, Middlesex EN2 6DD. Professional qualifications and information service.

Institute of Practitioners in Advertising, 44 Belgrave Square, London SW1X 8QS. Career information.

International Professional Security Association, 3 Dendy Road, Paignton, Devon TQ4 5DB. Tel: (01803) 554849.

Law Society's Careers and Recruitment Service, 227-228 Strand, London WC2R 1BA. Tel: (0171) 242 1222.

Library Association, 7 Ridgmount Street, London WC1E 7AE. Tel: (0171) 636 7543. Careers information.

Local Government Management Board, Arndale House, Arndale

Centre, Luton, Bedfordshire LU1 2TS. Tel: (01582) 451166. General information on administration and clerical work, working in promotional services, library and information services, financial services, legal services.
London Investment Banking Association, 6 Frederick Place, London EC2R 8BT. Tel: (0171) 796 3606. Careers information.
Managing and Marketing Sales Association Examination Board, PO Box 11, Sandbach, Cheshire. Tel: (0127) 077 339. Professional qualifications.
National Retail Training Council, Bedford House, 69-79 Fulham High Street, London SW6 3JW. Tel: (0171) 371 5021. Professional training and careers information.
Pensions Management Institute, PMI House, 4-10 Artillery Lane, London E1 7LS. Tel: (0171) 247 1452. Professional training.

Education and training
Association for the Education and Welfare of the Visually Handicapped, School of Education, University of Birmingham, PO Box 363, Birmingham B15 2TT. Tel: (0121) 414 4799. Specialist courses.
Central Council for Education and Training in Social Work, Derbyshire House, St Chad's Street, London WC1H 8AD. Tel: (0171) 278 2455. Information on education welfare work, professional qualifications.
Institute of Personnel and Development, IPD House, Camp Road, London SW19 4UX. Tel: (0181) 971 9000. Professional training and professional membership.
Local Government Management Board, Arndale House, Arndale Centre, Luton, Bedfordshire LU1 2TS. Tel: (01582) 451166. General information on working in personnel, training and development.
NATFHE, 27 Britannia Street, London WC1X 9JP. Union for university and college lecturers, supplies careers information.
Teaching as a Career Publicity Unit, 6th Floor, Sanctuary Buildings, Great Smith Street, London SW1P 3BT. Tel: (0171) 925 5880. Careers information.

Environment and animals
British Horse Society, British Equestrian Centre, Stoneleigh, Kenilworth, Warwickshire CV8 2LR. Tel: (01203) 696697. Professional training and professional membership.
Careers, Education and Training for Agriculture and the Country-

side, c/o Warwickshire Career Service, 10 Northgate Street, Warwick CV34 4SR. Tel: (01926) 412427.

Institute of Groundsmanship, 19-23 Church Street, The Agora, Wolverton, Milton Keynes, MK12 5LG. Tel: (01908) 312511. Professional training and professional membership.

Institute of Horticulture, 14-15 Belgrave Square, London SW1X 8PS. Tel: (0171) 245 6943. Careers information.

Landscape Institute, 6-7 Barnard Mews, London SW11 1QU. Tel: (0171) 738 9166. Careers information.

Local Government Management Board, Arndale House, Arndale Centre, Luton, Bedfordshire LU1 2TS. Tel: (01582) 451166. General information on working in environmental services, planning, architecture, landscape architecture, surveying, environmental health.

Royal Horticultural Society, 80 Vincent Square, Westminster, London SW1P 2PE. Tel: (0171) 834 4333. Professional qualifications.

Royal Institute of British Architects, 66 Portland Place, London W1N 4AD. Tel: (0171) 580 5533. Careers information and professional membership.

Royal Institute of Chartered Surveyors, Education and Training Department, Surveyor Court, Westwood Way, Coventry CV4 8JE. Tel: (0171) 222 7000.

Royal Town Planning Institute, 26 Portland Place, London W1N 4BE. Tel: (0171) 636 9107. Careers information and professional membership.

Health and beauty

Anglo-European College of Chiropractic, Parkwood Road, Bournemouth, Dorset BH5 2DF. Tel: (01202) 431021. Professional training.

Association of British Dispensing Opticians, 6 Hurlingham Business Park, Sulivan Road, London SW6 3DU. Tel: (0171) 736 0088. Careers information.

BMA Medical Education Trust, BMA House, Tavistock Square, London WC1H 9JP.

British Acupuncture Association and Register, 34 Alderney Street, London SW1V 4EY Tel: (0171) 834 6229.

British Association of Psychotherapists, 37 Mapesbury Road, London NW2 4HJ. Tel: (0181) 452 9823. Careers information.

British Association of Occupational Therapists, 6-8 Marshalsea Road, London SE1 1HL. Careers information.

British Association for Counselling, 1 Regent Place, Rugby,

Warwickshire CV21 2PJ. Tel: (01788) 578328. Careers information.
British College of Naturopathy and Osteopathy, Frazer House, 6 Netherhall Gardens, London NW3 5RR. Degree courses.
British Dietetic Association, 7th Floor, Elizabeth House, 22 Suffolk Street, Queensway, Birmingham B1 1LS. Tel: (0121) 643 5483. Careers information.
British Psychological Society, 48 Princess Road East, Leicester LE1 7DR. Tel: (01533) 549568. Professional training and professional membership.
British School of Osteopathy, 1-4 Suffolk Street, London SW1Y 4HG. Degree courses.
Chartered Society of Physiotherapy, 14 Bedford Row, London WC1R 4ED. Careers information.
College of Osteopaths, 13 Furzehill Road, Borehamwood, Hertfordshire WD6 2DG. Tel: (0181) 905 1937.
English National Board for Nursing, Midwifery and Health Visiting, Careers Information Centre, PO Box 356, Sheffield S8 0SJ.
European School of Osteopathy, 104 Tonbridge Road, Maidstone, Kent ME16 8SL.
Faculty of Homeopathy, The Royal London Homeopathic Hospital, Great Ormond Street, London WC1 3HR. Tel: (0171) 837 8833. Professional training.
General Dental Council, 37 Wimpole Street, London W1M 8DQ. Careers information.
Hairdressing Training Board, 3 Chequer Road, Doncaster DN1 2AA. Tel: (01302) 768262.
Health Education Authority, Hamilton House, Mabledon Place, London WC1H 9TX. Careers information.
Institute of Chiropodists, 27 Wright Street, Southport, Merseyside PR9 0TL. Tel: (01704) 546141. Careers information.
Institute of Electrolysis, Lansdowne House, 251 Seymour Grove, Manchester M16 0DS. Professional training.
Institute of Food Science and Technology, 5 Cambridge Court, 210 Shepherds Bush Road, London W6 7NL. Tel: (0171) 603 6316. Careers information.
International Health and Beauty Council, 46 Aldwick Road, Bognor Regis, West Sussex PO21 2PN. Professional qualifications.
International Therapy Examination Council (ITEC), James House, Oakelbrook Mill, Newent, Gloucestershire GL18 1HD. Tel: (01531) 821875. Professional training in beauty and complemen-

tary therapies.
London College of Osteopathic Medicine, 8-10 Boston Place, London NW1 6QH.
Medical Research Council, 20 Park Crescent, London W1N 4AL. Tel: (0171) 636 5422. Careers information.
National Institute of Medical Herbalists, 9 Palace Gate, Exeter EX1 1JA. Tel: (01392) 426022.
National Pharmaceutical Association, 38-42 St Peter's Square, St Albans, Hertfordshire AL1 3NP. Tel: (01727) 832161. Careers information.
Royal College of Surgeons in Edinburgh, Nicolson Street, Edinburgh EH8 9DW. Tel: (0131) 556 6206. Professional training in dentistry.
Royal College of Surgeons in England, 35-43 Lincoln's Inn Fields, London WC2A 3PN. Tel: (0171) 405 3474. Professional training in dentistry.
Royal Pharmaceutical Society of Great Britain, 1 Lambeth High Street, London SE1 7JN. Careers information.
Society of Apothecaries of London, Blackfriars Lane, London EC4V 6EJ. Tel: (0171) 236 1189. Professional training in pharmacy work.
Society of Chiropodists, 53 Welbeck Street, London W1M 7HE. Careers information.
Society of Homeopaths, 2 Artizan Road, Northampton NN1 4HU. Tel: (01604) 21400.

Leisure and tourism
Arts and Entertainment Training Council, Glyde House, Glydegate, Bradford, West Yorkshire BD5 0BQ. Tel: (01274) 738800.
British Institute of Innkeeping, 51-53 High Street, Camberley, Surrey GU15 3RG. Tel: (01276) 684449. Professional training and professional membership.
Council for Dance Education and Training, Riverside Studio, Crisp Road, London W6 9RL.
Hotel, Catering and Institutional Management Association, 191 Trinity Road, London SW17 7HN. Tel: (0181) 672 4251. Professional training and professional membership.
Institute of Leisure and Amenity Management, ILAM House, Lower Basildon, Reading, Berkshire RG8 9NE. Tel: (01491) 874222. Careers information in the leisure industry. SAE please.
Local Government Management Board, Arndale House, Arndale Centre, Luton, Bedfordshire LU1 2TS. Tel: (01582) 451166. General information on working in tourism, leisure services.

London Contemporary Dance School, 17 Duke's Road, London WC1H 9AB. Tel: (0171) 387 0152. Professional training.
London International Film School, 24 Shelton Street, Covent Garden, London WC2H 9HP. Tel: (0171) 836 9642. Professional training.
London School of Dance, 10 Linden Road, Bedford MK40 2DA. Tel: (01234) 213331. Professional training.
National Council for the Training of Journalists, Latton Bush Centre, Southern Way, Harlow, Essex CM18 7BL. Tel: (01279) 430009. Professional training.
Royal Academy of Dramatic Art, 62-64 Gower Street, London WC1E 6ED. Tel: (0171) 636 7076. Professional training.
Royal Ballet School, 155 Talgarth Road, London W14 9DE. Tel: (0181) 748 6335. Professional training.
Sports Council, 16 Upper Woburn Place, London WC1H 0QP. Tel: (0171) 388 1277. Information on professional qualification courses.
UK Council for Music Education and Training, 13 Back Lane, South Luffenham, Oakham, Leicester LE15 8NQ.

Science, engineering and IT
Association of Computer Professionals, 204 Barnett Wood Lane, Ashtead, Surrey KT21 2DB. Tel: (01372) 273442. Professional training and professional membership.
Chartered Institute of Building Service Engineers, 222 Balham High Road, London SW12 9BS. Careers information.
Electronics Examinations Board, Savoy Hill House, Savoy Hill, London WC2R 0BS. Tel: (0171) 826 3357.
Engineering Training Authority, Vector House, 41 Clarendon Road, Watford, Herts WD1 1HS. Tel: (freephone 0800 282167). Careers information.
Institute of Agricultural Engineers, Education and Careers Office, West End Road, Silsoe, Bedford MK45 4DU. Tel: (01525) 861096.
Institute of Brewing, 33 Clarges Street, London W1Y 8EE. Tel: (0171) 499 8144. Careers information.
Institute of Data Processing Management, IMDP House, Edgington Way, Ruxley Corner, Sidcup, Kent DA14 5HR. Tel: (0181) 308 0747. Professional training and professional membership.
Institute of Design Engineers, Courtleigh, Westbury Leigh, Westbury, Wiltshire BA13 3TA. Tel: (01373) 822801. Information.
Institute of Petroleum Information Service, 61 New Cavendish

Street, London W1M 8AR. Careers information.
Local Government Management Board, Arndale House, Arndale Centre, Luton, Bedfordshire LU1 2TS. Tel: (01582) 451166. General information on working in IT services, civil engineering.

Social care and protective services
Central Council for Education and Training in Social Work, Derbyshire House, St Chad's Street, London WC1H 8AD. Tel: (0171) 278 2455.
Community and Youth Work Association, 122 Rochdale Road, Oldham OL1 1NT. Tel: (0145) 783 4943. Professional qualifications and professional membership.
Council for Awards in Children's Care and Education, 8 Chequer Street, St Albans, Hertfordshire AL1 3XZ. Tel: (01727) 867609. Professional qualifications.
Institute of Career Guidance, 27a Lower High Street, Stourbridge DY8 1TA. Tel: (01384) 376464. Professional membership and careers guidance on being a careers officer.
Institute of Housing, Octavia House, Westwood Way, Westwood Business Park, Coventry CV4 8JP. Tel: (01203) 694433. Professional courses.
The Local Government Management Board, Arndale House, Arndale Centre, Luton, Bedfordshire LU1 2TS. Tel: (01582) 451166. General information on working in social services, housing and guidance services.
National Youth Agency, 17-23 Albion Street, Leicester LE1 6GD. Tel: (0116) 285 6789.
Society of Nursery Nursing Administrators Limited, 40 Archdale Road, East Dulwich, London SE22 9HJ. Tel: (0181) 299 2009. Professional qualifications and professional membership.

Index

A-levels, 32
access funds, 47
adult education, 41
APL, 81
application forms, 29
assessing competence, 82

balancing home and study, 54
basic education, 32, 90
benefits, 50
business schools, 88
building a support network, 57
building your portfolio, 84

career development loans, 51
case studies, 18, 29, 43, 52, 61, 71, 76, 85, 91, 98
Chamber of Commerce, 91
choosing a course, 37, 73
continuing education, centres of, 41
Council for the Accreditation of Correspondence Colleges (CACC), 73
CVs, 26

Department for Education and Employment, 46
discussion points, 18, 31, 44, 52, 62, 71, 76, 85, 92, 99

employer-led qualifications, 24

ESOL, 32
examining and awarding bodies, 33

family commitments, 54
finding a job with a future, 19
free training, 17, 48
freelancing, 14
further education, 33, 89

GCE (AS-Level), 32
GCSEs, 32
GNVQs, 38, 40

in-house training, 47
increasing confidence, 17, 57
industry-related training, 87
interviews, 29, 30

learning styles, 64
learning with young people, 54
local education authorities (LEA), 45
local enterprise agencies, 91

Management Initiative Charter (MIC), 88
mandatory grants, 46
marketing your skills, 26
mature student's allowance, 47
modern apprenticeships, 41
motivation, 65

Index

multi-skilling, 12
National Extension College (NEC), 74
networking, 56
non-qualification courses, 41
NVQs, 39, 77

open learning, 72
Open University (OU), 74
opportunities in
  business services and retail, 22
  education, teaching and training, 20
  environment and animals, 23
  health and beauty, 21
  leisure and tourism, 20
  science, engineering and IT, 23
  social care and protective services, 19

personal learning action plan, 93
private training, 90

qualifying for a university place, 35

residential colleges, 91

setting goals, 65
setting national standards, 79
solving problems, 67
special needs, 57
speculative letters, 27
student services, 57
students' union, 46
study skills, 63
studying at home, 75

telephone technique, 29
time management, 55
Training and Enterprise Councils (TECs), 46, 87
training at work, 17
training for work, 48

unemployment, 14
university, 35, 90
University of the Third Age, 61

vocational training, 19, 39
volunteering, 43

Workers' Educational Association (WEA), 42

youth credits, 49

Other titles in this series

CAREER NETWORKING
How to develop the right contacts to help you throughout your working life

Laurel Alexander

Unemployed? Redundant? Wanting promotion? – then career networking is for you. By systematically networking with other people, you can build bridges which could bring in offers of work. This book helps you take control of your working life through setting goals, assessing your networking needs and cultivating a supportive network. By working step-by-step through each practical chapter, you will understand how you can develop and plan your career through other people. Discover how you can be seen as a specialist selling something everyone wants using effective communication skills, assertive behaviour and being seen as a positive person. Learn how to network a room, how to gather information anywhere, from anyone. Do you know how to network using E-mail, the Internet and other technology? This books tells you how. There is further information on starting your own network, getting on other people's networks and extending your network. Laurel Alexander is a freelance trainer and consultant in career development and has helped many individuals improve their working life. She lives and works in Brighton, Sussex.

136p illus. 1 85703 350 7.

HOW TO START A NEW CAREER
Managing a better future for yourself

Judith Johnstone

More people than ever before are faced with big career changes today. Few if any jobs are 'for life'. Now in its second edition, this How To book helps you manage your entry into a new career effectively. It is aimed at anyone making a new start, whatever his or her age or background. It looks at who you are and what you are. It helps you evaluate your life skills, to recognise which careers you should concentrate on, and how to make a realistic plan for a happy and productive future. 'Written very much in the style of a work book, with practical exercises and pro formas for the student to complete...Well written – would be a useful addition to the library of any guidance practitioner working with adults.' *Newscheck/Careers Service Bulletin.*

140pp illus. 1 85703 139 3. 2nd edition.

How To Books

How To Books provide practical help on a large range of topics. They are available through all good bookshops or can be ordered direct from the distributors. Just tick the titles you want and complete the form on the following page.

- [ ] Apply to an Industrial Tribunal (£7.99)
- [ ] Applying for a Job (£8.99)
- [ ] Applying for a United States Visa (£15.99)
- [ ] Backpacking Round Europe (£8.99)
- [ ] Be a Freelance Journalist (£8.99)
- [ ] Be a Freelance Secretary (£8.99)
- [ ] Become a Freelance Sales Agent (£9.99)
- [ ] Become an Au Pair (£8.99)
- [ ] Becoming a Father (£8.99)
- [ ] Buy & Run a Shop (£8.99)
- [ ] Buy & Run a Small Hotel (£8.99)
- [ ] Buying a Personal Computer (£9.99)
- [ ] Career Networking (£8.99)
- [ ] Career Planning for Women (£8.99)
- [ ] Cash from your Computer (£9.99)
- [ ] Choosing a Nursing Home (£9.99)
- [ ] Choosing a Package Holiday (£8.99)
- [ ] Claim State Benefits (£9.99)
- [ ] Collecting a Debt (£9.99)
- [ ] Communicate at Work (£7.99)
- [ ] Conduct Staff Appraisals (£7.99)
- [ ] Conducting Effective Interviews (£8.99)
- [ ] Coping with Self Assessment (£9.99)
- [ ] Copyright & Law for Writers (£8.99)
- [ ] Counsel People at Work (£7.99)
- [ ] Creating a Twist in the Tale (£8.99)
- [ ] Creative Writing (£9.99)
- [ ] Critical Thinking for Students (£8.99)
- [ ] Dealing with a Death in the Family (£9.99)
- [ ] Do Voluntary Work Abroad (£8.99)
- [ ] Do Your Own Advertising (£8.99)
- [ ] Do Your Own PR (£8.99)
- [ ] Doing Business Abroad (£10.99)
- [ ] Doing Business on the Internet (£12.99)
- [ ] Emigrate (£9.99)
- [ ] Employ & Manage Staff (£8.99)
- [ ] Find Temporary Work Abroad (£8.99)
- [ ] Finding a Job in Canada (£9.99)
- [ ] Finding a Job in Computers (£8.99)
- [ ] Finding a Job in New Zealand (£9.99)
- [ ] Finding a Job with a Future (£8.99)
- [ ] Finding Work Overseas (£9.99)
- [ ] Freelance DJ-ing (£8.99)
- [ ] Freelance Teaching & Tutoring (£9.99)
- [ ] Get a Job Abroad (£10.99)
- [ ] Get a Job in America (£9.99)
- [ ] Get a Job in Australia (£9.99)
- [ ] Get a Job in Europe (£9.99)
- [ ] Get a Job in France (£9.99)
- [ ] Get a Job in Travel & Tourism (£8.99)
- [ ] Get into Radio (£8.99)
- [ ] Getting into Films & Television (£10.99)
- [ ] Getting That Job (£8.99)
- [ ] Getting your First Job (£8.99)
- [ ] Going to University (£8.99)
- [ ] Helping your Child to Read (£8.99)
- [ ] How to Study & Learn (£8.99)
- [ ] Investing in People (£9.99)
- [ ] Investing in Stocks & Shares (£9.99)
- [ ] Keep Business Accounts (£7.99)
- [ ] Know Your Rights at Work (£8.99)
- [ ] Live & Work in America (£9.99)
- [ ] Live & Work in Australia (£12.99)
- [ ] Live & Work in Germany (£9.99)
- [ ] Live & Work in Greece (£9.99)
- [ ] Live & Work in Italy (£8.99)
- [ ] Live & Work in New Zealand (£9.99)
- [ ] Live & Work in Portugal (£9.99)
- [ ] Live & Work in the Gulf (£9.99)
- [ ] Living & Working in Britain (£8.99)
- [ ] Living & Working in China (£9.99)
- [ ] Living & Working in Hong Kong (£10.99)
- [ ] Living & Working in Israel (£10.99)
- [ ] Living & Working in Saudi Arabia (£12.99)
- [ ] Living & Working in the Netherlands (£9.99)
- [ ] Making a Complaint (£8.99)
- [ ] Making a Wedding Speech (£8.99)
- [ ] Manage a Sales Team (£8.99)
- [ ] Manage an Office (£8.99)
- [ ] Manage Computers at Work (£8.99)
- [ ] Manage People at Work (£8.99)
- [ ] Manage Your Career (£8.99)
- [ ] Managing Budgets & Cash Flows (£9.99)
- [ ] Managing Meetings (£8.99)
- [ ] Managing Your Personal Finances (£8.99)
- [ ] Managing Yourself (£8.99)
- [ ] Market Yourself (£8.99)
- [ ] Master Book-Keeping (£8.99)
- [ ] Mastering Business English (£8.99)
- [ ] Master GCSE Accounts (£8.99)
- [ ] Master Public Speaking (£8.99)
- [ ] Migrating to Canada (£12.99)
- [ ] Obtaining Visas & Work Permits (£9.99)
- [ ] Organising Effective Training (£9.99)
- [ ] Pass Exams Without Anxiety (£7.99)
- [ ] Passing That Interview (£8.99)
- [ ] Plan a Wedding (£7.99)
- [ ] Planning Your Gap Year (£8.99)
- [ ] Prepare a Business Plan (£8.99)
- [ ] Publish a Book (£9.99)
- [ ] Publish a Newsletter (£9.99)
- [ ] Raise Funds & Sponsorship (£7.99)
- [ ] Rent & Buy Property in France (£9.99)
- [ ] Rent & Buy Property in Italy (£9.99)

How To Books

- Research Methods (£8.99)
- Retire Abroad (£8.99)
- Return to Work (£7.99)
- Run a Voluntary Group (£8.99)
- Setting up Home in Florida (£9.99)
- Spending a Year Abroad (£8.99)
- Start a Business from Home (£7.99)
- Start a New Career (£6.99)
- Starting to Manage (£8.99)
- Starting to Write (£8.99)
- Start Word Processing (£8.99)
- Start Your Own Business (£8.99)
- Study Abroad (£8.99)
- Study & Live in Britain (£7.99)
- Studying at University (£8.99)
- Studying for a Degree (£8.99)
- Successful Grandparenting (£8.99)
- Successful Mail Order Marketing (£9.99)
- Successful Single Parenting (£8.99)
- Survive Divorce (£8.99)
- Surviving Redundancy (£8.99)
- Taking in Students (£8.99)
- Taking on Staff (£8.99)
- Taking Your A-Levels (£8.99)
- Teach Abroad (£8.99)
- Teach Adults (£8.99)
- Teaching Someone to Drive (£8.99)
- Travel Round the World (£8.99)
- Understand Finance at Work (£8.99)
- Use a Library (£7.99)
- Use the Internet (£9.99)
- Winning Consumer Competitions (£8.99)
- Winning Presentations (£8.99)
- Work from Home (£8.99)
- Work in an Office (£7.99)
- Work in Retail (£8.99)
- Work with Dogs (£8.99)
- Working Abroad (£14.99)
- Working as a Holiday Rep (£9.99)
- Working in Japan (£10.99)
- Working in Photography (£8.99)
- Working in the Gulf (£10.99)
- Working in Hotels & Catering (£9.99)
- Working on Contract Worldwide (£9.99)
- Working on Cruise Ships (£9.99)
- Write a Press Release (£9.99)
- Write a Report (£8.99)
- Write an Assignment (£8.99)
- Write & Sell Computer Software (£9.99)
- Write for Publication (£8.99)
- Write for Television (£8.99)
- Writing a CV that Works (£8.99)
- Writing a Non Fiction Book (£9.99)
- Writing an Essay (£8.99)
- Writing & Publishing Poetry (£9.99)
- Writing & Selling a Novel (£8.99)
- Writing Business Letters (£8.99)
- Writing Reviews (£9.99)
- Writing Your Dissertation (£8.99)

To: Plymbridge Distributors Ltd, Plymbridge House, Estover Road, Plymouth PL6 7PZ. Customer Services Tel: (01752) 202301. Fax: (01752) 202331.

Please send me copies of the titles I have indicated. Please add postage & packing (UK £1, Europe including Eire, £2, World £3 airmail).

☐ I enclose cheque/PO payable to Plymbridge Distributors Ltd for £ _____

☐ Please charge to my ☐ MasterCard, ☐ Visa, ☐ AMEX card.

Account No. ☐☐☐☐ ☐☐☐☐ ☐☐☐☐ ☐☐☐☐

Card Expiry Date ☐☐ 19☐☐ ☎ **Credit Card orders may be faxed or phoned.**

Customer Name (CAPITALS) ....

Address ....

.... Postcode ....

Telephone .... Signature ....

Every effort will be made to despatch your copy as soon as possible but to avoid possible disappointment please allow up to 21 days for despatch time (42 days if overseas). Prices and availability are subject to change without notice.

Code BPA